ISBN 978-1-332-12049-9
PIBN 10287420

1 MONTH OF
FREE
READING

at

www.ForgottenBooks.com

By purchasing this book you are eligible for one month membership to ForgottenBooks.com, giving you unlimited access to our entire collection of over 1,000,000 titles via our web site and mobile apps.

To claim your free month visit:

www.forgottenbooks.com/free287420

English
Français
Deutsche
Italiano
Español
Português

www.forgottenbooks.com

Mythology Photography **Fiction**
Fishing Christianity **Art** Cooking
Essays Buddhism Freemasonry
Medicine **Biology** Music **Ancient
Egypt** Evolution Carpentry Physics
Dance Geology **Mathematics** Fitness
Shakespeare **Folklore** Yoga Marketing
Confidence Immortality Biographies
Poetry **Psychology** Witchcraft
Electronics Chemistry History **Law**
Accounting **Philosophy** Anthropology
Alchemy Drama Quantum Mechanics
Atheism Sexual Health **Ancient History**
Entrepreneurship Languages Sport
Paleontology Needlework Islam
Metaphysics Investment Archaeology
Parenting Statistics Criminology
Motivational

THE
DICTATOR

A Play in Three Acts

By

RICHARD HARDING DAVIS

Author of

"Soldiers of Fortune," "Ranson's Folly," "In the Fog,"
"Van Bibber," "Gallegher," &c.

New York
CHARLES SCRIBNER'S SONS

NEW YORK	LONDON
SAMUEL FRENCH	SAMUEL FRENCH, LTD.
PUBLISHER	26 SOUTHAMPTON STREET
25 WEST 45th STREET	STRAND, LONDON

THE DICTATOR

ALL RIGHTS RESERVED

THE DICTATOR

The CAST *of* THE DICTATOR *as presented* April 4, 1904, *by* CHARLES FROHMAN *at the* CRITERION THEATRE, New York.

THE PERSONS IN THE PLAY

BROOKE TRAVERS, alias "Steve" Hill..............William Collier

SIMPSON, his valet, alias "Jim" Dodd..............Edward Abeles

CHARLEY HYNE.... { wireless telegraph operator for the Red C Line } ...John Barrymore

COLONEL JOHN T. BOWIE.. { United States Consul at Porto Banos } ..George Nash

DUFFY, a secret-service detective...................Thomas McGrath

REV. ARTHUR BOSTICK.............................Henry J. West

LIEUTENANT PERRY, U. S. S. *Oregon*...............Thomas Meighan

SAMUEL CODMAN..... { Captain of the *Bolivar*, Red C Line } ....Emmett Whitney

GENERAL SANTOS CAMPOS ... { President of San Marana } ....Robert McWade, Jr.

DR. VASQUEZ, health officer at Porto Banos........Francis Sedgwick

SEÑOR JOSE DRAVO, proprietor of the Hotel del Prado....Louis Eagan

CORPORAL MANUEL.............................Wallace McCutcheon

COLONEL GARCIA, aide to General Campos.............Harry Senton

SMOKING-ROOM STEWARD.......................Augustus Goodson

LUCY SHERIDAN.................................Nanette Comstock

MRS. JOHN T. BOWIE.............................Lucille Watson

SEÑORA JUANITA ARGUILLA.........................Louise Allen

Soldiers, Sailors, Ship's Stewards, etc.

ACT I
Deck of the Steamer *Bolivar*, Harbor of Porto Banos.

ACT II
Three hours later. The Consulate of the United States, Porto Banos.

ACT III
Two hours later. The same.

TIME—The Present.

PLACE—Porto Banos, Republic of San Manana, Central America.

ACT I.

The scene shows the deck of the " Bolivar," a passenger steamer fitted for the tropics. The portion of the ship represented is as one looks across the deck from one rail to the other. Only the rail on the side of the ship farthest from the audience is seen. The back drop shows the harbor, and, at a distance of a quarter of a mile, the town of Porto Banos, with a line of cocoanut palms, wharves, white houses with red roofs, and yellow public buildings. Beyond the town is a high range of mountains. Running off the stage to the left is a superstructure in which are the passengers' cabins. In this, well on the stage, a cabin window and the door to the cabin face the audience. When this door is open one can see the interior of the cabin, with berths, a swinging lamp and a steamer trunk. On top of this superstructure is the office of the operator of the wireless telegraph. It looks like a chart room or covered companion way. Only a foot or two of it is in sight. The door in it is open toward the right, permitting the audience to see, issuing from inside the office, electric sparks and flashes, and to hear the sputtering of the instrument. An iron ladder runs down the side of the super-structure to the stage. Running off the stage to the right is a similar superstructure, which is the pas-sengers' smoking room. Outside the smoking room are set two wooden armchairs, painted white. Under the cabin window a steamer chair stretches toward the audience. The light is that of sunrise in the

tropics. It is supposed that the ship is just coming
to anchor.

At rise of the curtain CAPTAIN CODMAN, with his back
to the audience, is discovered leaning against the
rail. From the open door of the wireless office
come flashes of electric light and the buzzing of the
wireless.

CAPT. CODMAN.

(*Looking up, as though hailing some one above him and
off right.*) Mr. McKensie!

VOICE.

(*Off right.*) Aye, aye, sir!

CAPT. CODMAN.

(*Calling.*) Hold her where she is now. Stop her!

VOICE.

Aye, aye, sir! (*One bell sounds.*)

CAPT. CODMAN.

Lower away your anchors.

VOICE.

Forward there! Leg'go your anchors! (*The sound of
running anchor chains is heard and orders in a hoarse
voice from the distance still farther to the right.* CODMAN
*comes down. He is a bluff, red-faced, white-haired Cape
Cod sea captain. He wears an officer's blue cap and a white-
duck suit, around the sleeves of which are bands of tarnished
gold braid.* HYNE *has entered from office of wireless. He
is a young man of rather dissipated appearance. He
wears soiled duck trousers supported by a belt, a striped
linen shirt with pink garters around the sleeves, a handkerchief tucked inside his collar, and a duck yachting cap*

[4]

bearing the insignia of a ship's officer. His appearance is that of a man who has been up all night.)

CAPT. CODMAN.

Well—did you get my "wireless" through?

HYNE.

(*From upper deck descends ladder to stage.*) No; there's nobody at the other end.

CAPT. CODMAN.

Ain't you going to try any more?

HYNE.

What's the use of trying when there's nobody there? The only sure way to get a wireless telegram through— that I know—is to take it ashore in a rowboat.

CAPT. CODMAN.

Well, you *ought* to know how to do it. The company pays you to do it——

HYNE.

If the company paid me for *all* the work I did, I wouldn't have to work. I agreed to come down here and take charge of that wireless station (*points toward* Porto Banos), and you've made me do the work of three men.

CAPT. CODMAN.

Well, the chief steward's ill, and the doctor can't leave his berth.

HYNE.

Yes, and I've been purser, barkeeper, medical man.
"Bo'sun tight, an' the midshipmite,
And the crew of the Captain's gig."
Been mixing medicines, mixing drinks, and now I got the company's account mixed. (*Crosses right.*)

[5]

CAPT. CODMAN.

If you didn't mix so many drinks you wouldn't mix your accounts.   Send the boy to my cabin with my coffee.

HYNE.

Yes, sir!   (*Calling into smoking room.*)   Steward!

CAPT. CODMAN.

And you better drink something yourself.

HYNE.

(*Turns with a smile of assent and anticipation.*)   Yes, sir!

CAPT. CODMAN.

Coffee (HYNE'S *face drops*)—no more swizzles.   (*Goes up stage and looks over bulwark rail.*)

HYNE.

No, sir.   (STEWARD *appears at door of smoking room.*) Captain wants his coffee in his cabin.

STEWARD.

(*Crosses left.*)   Yes, sir.   Anything for you, sir?

HYNE.

(*Virtuously.*)   No.   (*In a whisper.*)   A Manhattan.

STEWARD.

(*In a whisper.*)   All right, sir!   (*Goes off left.*)

CAPT. CODMAN.

(*Coming down and taking up thread of former conversation.*)   There's been too much drinking this trip—and too much poker-playing.   I'm glad some of these passengers are going ashore.   Two of 'em is card sharps.

HYNE.

Really? Which two, sir?

CAPT. CODMAN.

You know 'em well enough. Those New York sports, that came over the side just as we sailed.

HYNE.

Mr. "Steve" and Mr. "Jim"?

CAPT. CODMAN.

(*Mysteriously.*) That's what they call each other in the smoking room, but one night in front of the wheel-house, when they didn't know I was inside, they called each other very different names——

HYNE.

Called each other names, did they?

CAPT. CODMAN.

Called each other Mr. This and Mr. That—very stiff and polite.

HYNE.

Well, any purser that sails for these ports has got to take any name the passenger chooses to give him.

CAPT. CODMAN.

Oh, I make allowances, but that Mr. Steve is a rascal! You might think this was *his* yacht, might think *I* was his sailing master. "Old Salt," he calls *me*. "Hello, Old Salt!" he says. I give him a good answer yesterday. When he says "Good morning, Old Salt," I says "Good morning, young Fresh," I says. (*Chuckles.*) My first officer, he laughed fit to choke when I says that.

HYNE.

(*Morosely.*) Yes—*he* would. Sort of a joke that first officer would laugh at—when the Captain makes it.

CAPT. CODMAN.

(*Turning on* HYNE.) See here! don't you be too familiar or you'll lose your job.

HYNE.

I wouldn't mind losing *two* of my jobs. I tell you, I'm doing the work of three men now.

CAPT. CODMAN.

You can't do the work of one man if you spend all your time in the smoking room with them—rascals. I see you, especially with the little one that looks like he seen a ghost.

HYNE.

I don't recognize him. Which is he?

CAPT. CODMAN.

Why, the one that (points *left*)—*that* one. (*Moves right.*) Hurry up that coffee! (*He goes off below the smoking room.*)

HYNE.

Yes, sir. (*Turns to go left, but stops when he sees* JIM SIMPSON, *or* "JIM," *enter lower left.* JIM *is a young English-lishman, smooth-shaven, and with the deferential air of a servant. He has a nervous, frightened manner, and is neatly but plainly dressed in a single-breasted suit of blue serge, golf cap, and tan shoes.*)

JIM.

Good morning.

HYNE.

Good morning.

JIM.

Why have the engines stopped?

HYNE.

I guess that engineer forgot to wind them up last night. (*Turns and points at* Porto Banos.) Look where you are.

JIM.

(*Turning and looking toward the land.*) Why, we're *there!* From my side of the ship you can't see anything but water. (STEWARD *enters lower left, bearing tray with coffee cup and cocktail glass, crossing down right in front of* HYNE.)

HYNE.

(*To* STEWARD, *when he has passed him.*) Here, that's mine! (*To* JIM.) Have a drink?

JIM.

No, thanks.

HYNE.

You better.

JIM.

No, thanks, it's too early.

HYNE.

(*Taking the cocktail.*) It's never too *early* for a drink. It may be too *late.* (*Drinks.*) You're too late for that one. (*Returns glass;* STEWARD *goes off right.*)

JIM.

(*Coming down.*) And—and is that Porto Banos?

[9]

HYNE.

Yes—and it's the hottest and unhealthiest hole south of Yucatan. And that's where I got to live the rest of my life, unless I win out by dying of yellow fever.

JIM.

I thought your job was on the ship—to run the wireless and run errands, and——

HYNE.

No—I been promoted—to that fever swamp. We've got our wireless station in the consulate. Our operator moved in the day the last Consul died of yellow fever; the next day the operator died. I wonder which will be the next one to go. You—or I—or Mr. Steve.

JIM.

(*Looking about him timidly, and moving nearer to Hyne.*)
Well, Mr. Steve—Steve and I were talking it over last night and we think we don't want to go to Porto Banos.

HYNE.

Don't want to go? But you're there! Why didn't you think of that before you left New York?

JIM.

Well, you see, in New York the doctor—the doctor ordered Mr. Steve to take a sea voyage—for his health; but we left so suddenly we—we hadn't time to choose.

HYNE.

Well, then, why don't you go on with the ship to Jamaica? That's a healthy place.

JIM.

I—I'm afraid it wouldn't be healthy for Mr. Steve. You see, there's a cable to Jamaica.

HYNE.

Yes, and there's a wireless to Porto Banos.

JIM.

(*Ingratiatingly.*) Ah! But if *you* got messages disturbing Mr. Steve, maybe you'd let him know?

HYNE.

What?

JIM.

(*Hurriedly.*) I mean that the doctor wants him to rest, he wants him to get away from cables and Wall Street reports, and——

HYNE.

Oh, we carry a lot of that trade!

JIM.

I beg your pardon?

HYNE.

I say, we carry a lot of passengers who leave New York for their *health*. (*Familiarly.*) Look here, why don't you two children put me next? I'm no correspondence school, but if I could meet you face to face I could help you two. (JIM *turns as though to confide in* HYNE, *and then shakes his head.*)

JIM.

(*Sadly.*) No. But don't think we don't appreciate your offer.

HYNE.

Oh, that's all right! I'm dead sorry for you two, you're so helpless. You're the original babes in the woods, that's what you are. You two could play *Little Eva* and *Lord Fauntleroy* without making up.

[11]

JIM.

(*Fearfully.*) Who's said anything about us to make you think that——

HYNE.

(*Laughs scornfully.*) Who? Why, you give yourselves away! You're such amateurs! Now, I'm a wise guy. I'm not like some folks. I can tell where the third rail is without walking on it. (*After a pause, encouragingly.*) Better take mother's advice.

JIM.

(*Uncertainly.*) Well—well—Mr. Steve told me if I was sure you suspected—(HYNE *laughs*)—I'll do this! I'll tell you what happened to two men I know in New York, and you can tell me what's likely to happen to them in Porto Banos.

HYNE.

(*Warningly.*) Don't say anything you'll be sorry for in the morning.

JIM.

No! I'll be careful.

HYNE.

I don't want your telephone number unless you want to give it, understand?

JIM.

Yes, I think I do. (*Glances about him, and then speaks in a nervous whisper.*) A week ago in New York, just after midnight, a gentleman with his valet left his house to go aboard his yacht at the New York Yacht Club's wharf at Twenty-third Street. They called up a cab in the street, put their trunks on it, and drove to the East River. The pier was dark, there was no one about, so the cabman soaked them ten dollars for the trip. The gentleman refused to pay it, and the cabman soaked him. He struck back, and the cabman fell—hitting his head on the curbstone. Did you ever meet one of those New York curbstones?

HYNE.

(*Nods impatiently.*) Go on.

JIM.

Then you can imagine what happened to that cabman's head.

HYNE.

Gee!

JIM.

A crowd of roughs collected and accused the gentleman of trying to murder the cabman. Then the ambulance surgeon came, and he said the cabman could live only a very short time, and advised these men to leave the country in an *even shorter time.* They took his advice, and the cab with the trunks on it, and galloped to the wharf of the Red C Line—where this ship was bound for Central America. They didn't care *where* she was bound for, so long as she—bounded. Now they have arrived at Porto Banos, and this is where *you* could assist them. (*Earnestly*) Is there an extradition treaty between the United States and this Republic, and if these men go on shore can they be dragged back to New York?

HYNE.

I don't know about *this* Republic, but I'll bet you after you've been in Porto Banos a couple of hours you won't need an extradition treaty to get you to go home again.

JIM.

But is there a treaty?

[13]

HYNE.

I don't know.

JIM.

Well, who would know?

HYNE.

Why, Colonel Bowie.

JIM.

The Consul?

HYNE.

Well, he's going to be the Consul. He's never been here before, but he's lived in every other Republic in Central America, and he must know all about this one, or he wouldn't have pulled wires so hard to get this consular job. *He's* the man to ask.

(STEWARD *enters* right, *and salutes* HYNE.)

STEWARD.

Mr. Hyne, the Captain says to tell you the Health Officer is leaving the wharf.

HYNE.

All right. Ask the ship's doctor to have his health bill ready for me.

STEWARD.

Yes, sir. (*Goes off left.*)

HYNE.

There's more work to do! Come and have a drink with the Health Officer and me. (*Moves left.* COLONEL BOWIE *with* MRS. BOWIE *on his left arm enters from above cabin. They stand at the rail while he points out to her the features of Porto Banos. He is a tall, important-looking man, with a low-crowned Panama hat, black goatee, and gray frock coat. At times his manner is that of a political demagogue and again that of a sharp rascal. MRS. BOWIE is young, pretty, and silly. She is overdressed in what obviously is part of the trousseau of a bride.)*

JIM.

(*Peevishly.*) No, I just said I wouldn't drink. You drink more than a man should.

HYNE.

But not more than *three* men should. I'm the doctor now. It was the purser got that last drink. (*Turns and discovers* BOWIE.) There's the Consul. Now, my advice to your two friends is that you ask *him* about that extradition law.

JIM.

(*Frightened.*) No—not while his wife's with him—and I've got to call Mr. Steve at four bells.

HYNE.

You've plenty of time. Come with me, and I'll introduce you to the Health Officer. You can ask *him* about that extradition.

JIM.

(*Terrified.*) But we mustn't ask *everybody*. They'll wonder why we want to know.

HYNE.

Not in this country. It's the first question every American asks. (*Leads* JIM *off left.* CAPTAIN *enters below smoking room, looks after* JIM, *scowling.*)

BOWIE.

Ah, Captain.

CAPT. CODMAN.

Good morning, Mr. Consul. Good morning, Mrs. Bowie.

BOWIE.

(*Pompously.*) My dear, thank the Captain who brought us safely through the perils of the deep to our new home. I congratulate you, Captain. You carried a precious cargo.

CAPT. CODMAN.

No, this trip mostly hardware.

BOWIE.

The precious cargo to which I referred, Captain, was my young bride.

CAPT. CODMAN.

Oh, excuse me, marm! An' how do you think you'll like your new home, Mrs. Bowie? That's it! (Points *to* Porto *Banos.*) The consulate is part of that hotel.

MRS. BOWIE.

Well, I've made up my mind to like whatever my husband likes. Haven't I, John?

BOWIE.

Yes, dear.

CAPT. CODMAN.

That's right! I guess, Consul, it's no new home to you?

BOWIE.

Well, it is, and it isn't. I've never been *here* before——

CAPT. CODMAN.

No?

BOWIE.

No, but for the last ten years I've lived in every other Republic in Central America, and I feel at home in any of 'em.

CAPT. CODMAN.

Just so! But I should have thought you'd have got a consulship in a place where you were acquainted already—been more sociable for Mrs. Bowie.

BOWIE.

Yes, but between ourselves, Captain, a Consul must keep clear of local politics, and wherever *I've* been in Central America I've prominently identified myself with one or the other of the political parties. I was *against* the government in Guatemala, in Costa Rica I was *with* it. In Salvadore I *was* the government.

CAPT. CODMAN.

You don't say?

BOWIE.

Yes, I've been mixed up in the revolutions of every Republic in Central America.

MRS. BOWIE.

(*Quickly.*) Except this one, John

BOWIE.

Yes, of course, except this one. So when the State Department begged me to represent my country in a diplomatic post, I chose Porto Banos because there I have no interest—except to serve that flag. (*Raises his hat and looks up apparently at the mast head.*)

CAPT. CODMAN.

(*Thoughtfully*). Quite so! quite so! I guess you must

be the Colonel Bowie who—why, this very ship once carried a cargo of rifles for you to——

BOWIE.

(*Airily.*) Very likely! very likely!

CAPT. CODMAN.

I see! Well, Consul, I think you're quite right to come to a place where you start with a clean ticket, where you haven't plotted to upset their little government. (*To* MRS. BOWIE.) Excuse me, I'll see you before you leave the ship. (*He goes off. There is a pause, during which* MR. *and* MRS. BOWIE *look at each other, smiling.*)

MRS. BOWIE.

John, I'm glad—I'm glad you didn't "plot to upset their little government." (*They both laugh knowingly.*)

BOWIE.

Yes, that would have been mean of me, wouldn't it? (*Points at* Porto Banos, *speaking grandiloquently.*) Julia, there is my wedding gift to you. You are mistress of all you survey.

MRS. BOWIE.

Oh, John! And my friends thought I was doing so well to marry an American Consul.

BOWIE.

Hah! what's a Consul in San Manana compared to the Dictator of San Manana? Julia, you will be the first lady of the land!

MRS. BOWIE.

My, that sounds nice! Will my social position be higher than that of the wife of the President of San Manana?

[18]

BOWIE.

Than Rivas's wife? Who made Rivas President?

MRS. BOWIE.

You did, John.

BOWIE.

And who can unmake Rivas?

MRS. BOWIE.

(*Admiringly.*) I guess you can, John.

BOWIE.

Then his wife had better keep her place—or he'll lose his. I found Pedro Rivas in New York. Sent him back to his country—and made him President. My brains. My money. They (*nods toward the shore*) think I'm only the new American Consul, but when they go to Rivas for a concession, he'll say, "Have you seen Bowie?" I'm Dictator of that Republic and he knows it. I'm the king-maker, the Warwick, the man behind the throne. Pedro Rivas can be President, but Col. John T. Bowie is Boss.

MRS. BOWIE.

Oh, John, but you do talk elegant! I'm *glad* you're boss, and I'm glad we've come to boss a country where they don't know you.

BOWIE.

(*Dryly.*) So am I. But why are you glad?

MRS. BOWIE.

Oh, John, I'm just jealous of the people you knew down here before you met me. Those beautiful *señoritas*——

BOWIE.

(*Warningly.*) Now, Julia——

MRS. BOWIE.

(*Pouting.*) Well, I can't help it. I can't forget that Panama widow—Juanita something.

BOWIE.

Now, Julia, why should you be jealous of a woman I ran away from—in order to marry you?

MRS. BOWIE.

Well, I *am* jealous—and I don't like those you've met *since* you married me either. I don't like that missionary girl.

BOWIE.

(*Wearily.*) *Who* is it now? Miss Sheridan—the young lady that came down with us——?

MRS. BOWIE.

I just hate her. I don't think a nice girl would travel alone, even if she is going to marry a missionary.

BOWIE.

Why, she's under the Captain's care on board, and on shore she's——

MRS. BOWIE.

Under your care, yes.

BOWIE.

Well, the Board of Missionaries put her in charge of the Consul. I didn't. (*The bell of a launch sounds off at upper right.* BOWIE *goes up and looks over the rail.*)

MRS. BOWIE.

That girl has just spoiled my trip. If she wanted to save the heathen, why didn't she stay in New York. And the way she's been carrying on with that Mr. Steve is shocking. (HYNE *and* JIM *enter and halt at corner of cabin.*)

BOWIE.

Well, she hasn't been carrying on with me. (*To* HYNE.) My, Hyne, who is that in the launch?

HYNE.

Health Officer. (*To* JIM.) Are you going to ask him now?

JIM.

No, I am going to wake Mr. Steve; maybe he'd rather ask Bowie himself.

HYNE.

All right, suit yourself. (*Goes off upper right.*)

MRS. BOWIE.

(*In a whisper. Looking over rail.*) Is that one of your men, John?

BOWIE.

I can't tell until he gives me the sign. Let's go find out.

MRS. BOWIE.

He doesn't know you're his boss, does he?

BOWIE.

Not yet. But if there's any graft in being a Health Officer, he soon will. (*They go off behind smoking room.* JIM *looks after them, glances cautiously about the deck, and then knocks on window of cabin.*)

JIM.

Mr. Travers! Mr. Travers! (STEVE *enters from door*

of cabin. He is an alert young man of twenty-five, wearing white-duck trousers and the coat and cap of the New York Yacht Club.)

STEVE.

(Sharply.) I told you *not* to say Mr. Travers, but to call me "Steve."

JIM.

Yes, Mr. Steve.

STEVE.

And I told you *not* to call me till we got to Porto Banos.

JIM.

But we're there, sir! This is Porto Banos.

STEVE.

(Eagerly.) Is it? What's it like? Is it—is it the sort of place I'd select to spend the rest of my life in?

JIM.

I can't say, sir.

STEVE.

Well, *don't* say "sir." I told you *not* to say "sir."

JIM.

No, sir.

STEVE.

Now listen! Do you want to be hanged?

JIM.

No, Mr. Travers.

STEVE.

(Correcting him.) No, "Steve."

JIM.

(Respectfully.) No—Steve.

[22]

STEVE.

Don't say it that way; say it as though you meant it. I ask you, "Do you want to get hanged?" And you say, "No, Steve." Say "No, Steve," cheerfully. Don't be afraid of it. "No, Steve," like that. (*Slaps him on the back.*) Like that! You *don't* want to be hanged, do you?

JIM.

No—Steve?

STEVE.

Cheerfully. Slap me on the back, go on! (JIM *timidly taps* STEVE *on the shoulder.*)

JIM.

No, Steve.

STEVE.

That's better. Now listen! I'm sorry you had to come here, but it was for your good as well as mine. If I'd left you behind you'd have gone to jail, and I—I'd have had to clean my own boots. And shave myself. I can't shave myself, can I?

JIM.

No, sir. No—Steve.

STEVE.

I can't sharpen razors, nor—nor do any of those things you're so clever at. I've *got* to have a valet. But people mustn't *know* you're a valet. That would identify both of us. "Wanted by the New York Police," that's the way it probably reads: "Mr. Brooke Travers and Valet." Why, Simpson——

JIM.

(*Correcting him.*) "Jim."

STEVE.

Thank you. (*Takes* JIM'S *arm and walks across to*

right.) Now please remember, Jim, that I'm your old college friend Stephen Hill. Steve! Good old Steve! And you're just as good as I am—and when anybody's about—you're better. (*Stops.*) Except when Miss Sheridan's about, and then, you're not to be about.

JIM.

(*Gloomily.*) Yes, Steve. (STEVE *turns*—JIM *corrects himself and in a jaunty manner takes* STEVE *by the arm.*) Yes, Steve.

STEVE.

That's right. Now then bring on your Porto Banos. (*Turns and looks toward the land.*) Is that it?

JIM.

Yes, sir. The purser says it looks much better at night.

STEVE.

I should think it might on a dark night. However, it's any port in a storm with us. Did you find out if what the man said about the extradition law was true?

JIM.

Not yet, sir, the purser told me to ask Colonel Bowie, the Consul.

STEVE.

(*Thoughtfully.*) Bowie. Yes, he'd know, but he'd suspect. He talks like a fool, but he's no fool. He's a rascal. Still, it's all the better for us that he is a rascal. Now the Consul will have more to say about extraditing us than anybody else and we've got to make it worth his while not to say it. We will be the geese that lay the golden eggs for the Consul, and he mustn't kill the geese.

JIM.

Yes, sir.

STEVE.

(*Turning on him.*) "Yes, sir," and you don't know what I mean at all.

JIM.

No, sir.

STEVE.

I mean that every week that we remain free he gets his gold, but that if he lets them take us back to the United States—he loses his gold. Now you go tell Bowie—tell him everything, he's the only one can help us. Do you understand?

JIM.

Yes, sir.

(Two STEWARDS cross *from upper left to upper right carrying between them a cabin trunk. LUCY SHERIDAN enters upper left, adjusting a marine binocular. She raises it to her eyes and stands at the rail looking off. She is an attractive girl, in a white skirt, shirt waist, and stock, and with a puggaree around a man's gray sombrero.*)

JIM.

(*Sees* LUCY.) Be careful, sir.

STEVE.

Who is it?

JIM.

(*In a whisper.*) Miss Sheridan.

STEVE.

Look out. (*Aloud.*) No, Jim, old man, let *me* pack the trunks this time, let me pack the trunks. (LUCY, *hearing voices, turns and comes down.*) Go on.

JIM.

(*With hysterical gayety.*) No—Steve, I couldn't think

of it. No, no, old—old chappie. (*Gives him pokes in ribs.*)

STEVE.

(*Aside.*) That's good, that's all right. (*Aloud.*) No, I insist, I'll toss you for it. (*Takes out a half a dollar.*) What? Miss Sheridan? (*Turns to her.*) Oh, good morning, Miss Sheridan.

LUCY.

Good morning. (*She nods to* JIM, *he bows.*)

STEVE.

We were just quarreling over who would pack the trunks. Jim is *so* unselfish. He always wants to pack the trunks. But I'm unselfish too, so we're going to toss for it. (*To* JIM.) Heads or tails.

JIM.

Heads.

STEVE.

Tails, it is. You lose. You pack the trunks. Isn't it funny how you always lose? (*Aside.*) Go tell Bowie. Tell him everything. He's the only man who can save us.

JIM.

Yes, sir. (*He exits upper right.* LUCY *and* STEVE, *appreciating that they soon are to separate, approach each other with mutual embarrassment.*)

STEVE.

Well?

LUCY.

Well?

STEVE.

(*Mournfully.*) Well, here we are. I'm glad.

[26]

LUCY.

(*Sadly.*) So am I.

STEVE.

(*Trying to appear at ease.*) I've never seen Porto Banos. I've seen every other foreign port in the world, Naples and—Naples, but I've never seen Porto Banos. Of course it's different with you. I travel for pleasure. That's why I came to Porto Banos. But you must go where duty calls you. How many little heathen are there in Porto Banos?

LUCY.

(*Wearily turning away.*) Oh, please don't joke about it! I don't—I don't feel very gay this morning. I'm afraid I'm a little homesick.

STEVE.

Oh, I'm sorry! But you'll soon get over that. (*Resentfully.*) You'll soon make this place your home. And in a few minutes Mr. ——, I never can remember the name of that young man you are going to marry.

LUCY.

Mr. Bostick.

STEVE.

Bostick, of course. He'll be coming out in a few minutes now, and that will be one friendly face to greet you. No one's coming out to meet me. (*He turns hastily, and gazes with alarm toward the wharf.*) At least, I hope not. (STEWARD *enters.*)

STEWARD.

(*Saluting* LUCY.) Beg pardon, Miss, Health Officer says passengers can go ashore, now. The boat's waiting.

LUCY.

Thanks.

STEWARD.

(*To* STEVE.)   Your cabin pieces ready, sir?

STEVE.

I don't know.   Ask my—ask Mr. Jim.

STEWARD.

Yes, sir.   Have you seen the Boots, sir?

STEVE.

No, I haven't seen any boots.   Has somebody lost his boots?

STEWARD.

I'm the " Boots," sir; I'm the man that cleans the boots.

STEVE.

(*Gives him money.*)   You mean you're the man that doesn't clean the boots.   Now, go tell the Captain to come here.   I want to tip him, too.   (STEWARD *exits.*)   I've tipped every other man on board this boat, and if I didn't tip him, it would hurt his feelings.   (*Turning to* LUCY.) What sort of a chap is Bostick—I mean, of course, he's a bully fine fellow or you wouldn't marry him.   But I mean is he a sort of a sport, or is he a serious chap—some of those missionaries, you know, rather go in for being serious.

LUCY.

Yes, he's serious, and Mr. Bostick is very *good.*

STEVE.

(*Encouragingly.*)   Yes, and——?

LUCY.

And very *earnest.*

[28]

STEVE.

Oh, that's where I'm weak. I'm terribly shy on earnestness. And—and—what else—about Bostick?

LUCY.

That's all. I don't know Mr. Bostick very well.

STEVE.

You don't know him very well!

LUCY.

He wrote to the Board of Missions that he thought his influence with the Carib Indians would be greater if he were a married man.

STEVE.

Well?

LUCY.

So when he came North they called for volunteers among the young girls who wished to be missionaries, and Mr. Bostick and I met, and talked it over, and found we were in sympathy, and so I have come down to marry him. (*There is a pause.*)

STEVE.

See here, my dear young lady, don't you think you are taking pretty big chances? Of course, it's none of my business——

LUCY.

(*Severely.*) As you say, it is none of your business.

STEVE.

That's what I said, I said it was none of my business, but if you're looking for a heathen to save, you needn't marry a man you don't know, nor climb those mountains to find him. Look at me! Look at the good you've done me. Just on this trip! I'm a better man for it. My dear Miss Sheridan, I don't want to interfere with your matrimonial engagements, but I hate' to see a nice girl bury herself for life in a Central American banana patch. Nice girls are very few, and they're getting married to some *other* fellow every day. A nice girl could do wonders with me. She could save me.

LUCY.

(*Turning and smiling at him.*) I ought to be angry with you, but I'm not—because you are not serious—you never are serious.

STEVE.

But I am serious. Don't you think I'm worth saving? (DUFFY enters *from left. Through* LUCY'S *next speech he tries to attract the attention of* LUCY *and* STEVE *by hissing at them. He is a stupid, fatuous, self-important person, with an air of mystery. He is heavily built, and his mustache is black. He wears a suit of ready-made imitation tweed, a gray alpine hat with a black band and the rim pulled down in front.*)

LUCY.

What is there to save you from—except yourself? You have everything. What is there to save you from?

DUFFY.

Hist! Hist! (STEVE *and* LUCY *turn and discover* DUFFY.)

STEVE.

(*Points at* DUFFY.) Well, you might save me from that!

DUFFY.

Hush! Don't tell anybody. (*In a very loud voice.*) I am a secret-service detective.

STEVE.

(*Terrified.*) You're a what? What does he say he is?

DUFFY.

I'm a secret-service detective. I was in Porto Rico on government business. They cabled me from New York to come here. Do you doubt it? (*Reaches inside the arm-hole of his waistcoat.*) Do you want to see my badge?

STEVE.

(*Violently.*) No, I don't want to see your badge. Take your badge away. Do you want to frighten the lady? (*To* LUCY, *who is amused by* DUFFY's *manner.*) What are you frightened about? What's the use of being frightened? If you have a clear conscience, you needn't— (*To* DUFFY.) What do you want?

DUFFY.

I want you to assist me—in the name of the law. I'm looking for two men.

STEVE.

(*Falling back.*) Two men! Well, we're not two men, man and woman. (*Pointing to* LUCY.) Woman! (*To himself.*) Man! (*To* LUCY.) The idea of a secret cir-cus—secret circus! (*Slowly.*) Not secret circus—secret-service detective not being able to tell two men from a man and a woman. It's absurd!

DUFFY.

Don't delay me! Where is the Captain of this ship?

STEVE.

(*With delight.*) The Captain. Oh, the Captain! (*Taking* DUFFY *by arm and leading him* right.) I'll assist you to find the Captain. (*Points to lower right.*) He is right down there, right along that alley way.

DUFFY.

(*Moving right.*) Thank you—don't tell anybody I'm a secret-service detective.

STEVE.

Not for worlds. See that open hatch, the Captain's down that hatch. Jump down three decks—and turn to the right. (*Exit* DUFFY.) (STEVE *turns excitedly to* LUCY.) Excuse me, but I've got to see Colonel Bowie. (*She moves up stage left, he following.*) This is very serious. Somebody is going to be arrested. A fellow-passenger, perhaps a fellow-mortal. You, *you*, go save the heathen, but I will save my fellow-passengers. Excuse me, won't you? (*Shakes her hand absent-mindedly.*)

LUCY.

Then this is good-by, or— (*Wistfully.*) Will I see you on shore?

STEVE.

(*Violently.*) You *bet* you'll see me on shore. I'll be on shore before you are, if I have to swim. (*Runs down to lower right.*)

LUCY.

Au revoir, then.

STEVE.

Don't mention it. (LUCY *exits behind cabin, as* JIM *comes on from behind smoking room.*) Did you tell Bowie?

JIM.

Yes, sir; everything.

STEVE.

What did he say?

JIM.

Said accidents would happen.

[32]

STEVE.

Did he try to blackmail you?

JIM.

No, sir!

STEVE.

He didn't! Then he must know *I'm* the one that's got the money. Go pack the trunks, I'll fix him. (JIM *exits into the cabin as* COLONEL BOWIE *enters lower right*)

BOWIE.

Well! What can I do for you? Your servant tells me——

STEVE.

Has he told you about those two young men?

BOWIE.

Yes; they're in a pretty bad fix.

STEVE.

But he hasn't told you the *worst*. (BOWIE *turns to sit.* STEVE *prevents him from doing so.*) You haven't time to sit down. There is a secret-service detective here from Porto Banos. He is trying to arrest those two young men.

BOWIE.

Indeed, that is *unfortunate*!

STEVE.

I know that. You don't have to tell me that. What I want to know is this—is there any extradition treaty with this country, and if so, are you going to allow these innocent young men to be dragged back to New York on a charge of murder—and hanged?

BOWIE.

(*Judicially*.)   Well, in the first place——

STEVE.

Wait!   Before you commit yourself, you ought to know that on the day these two young men fled, one of them had been to the races and had taken from the bookmakers twenty-five thousand dollars in cash—no credit—cash! And he has it with him now.   (*He shows a bank-note case filled with* notes.   Bowie *regards it greedily*.)   I thought that might have an international bearing on the subject.

BOWIE.

You're right, it *has!*   Well, there *is* an extradition treaty with San Manana.

STEVE.

There is?

BOWIE.

But——

STEVE.

(*Delightedly*.)   But!

BOWIE.

But let us suppose that the Consul—before which this case must come—had met your friends on the way down—had taken a fancy to them—had lost some five hundred dollars to them at poker, for which they held his I. O. U.'s.

STEVE.

Oh, don't mention it.

BOWIE.

And that he has inclined to be their friend.

STEVE.

Good, old Bowie!

[34]

BOWIE.

In that case he might fail to recognize his friends as the men described in the extradition papers——

STEVE.

He might, he could. (*Takes bundle of papers from his inside pocket, and gives it to* BOWIE.) Allow me. Some I. O. U.'s of yours——

BOWIE.

(*Taking papers.*) Thank you. Now listen. I am told that the consulate is situated in a wing of the Hotel del Prado. I will furnish you with rooms in the hotel, so that you will be near me in case I have to warn you. You will pay the rent of the rooms to *me*.

STEVE.

(*Winking.*) I see.

BOWIE.

Five hundred dollars a week.

STEVE.

Five—five hundred dollars! Did you ever think that it takes a long time to earn five hundred dollars?

BOWIE.

Did you ever think that it takes a long time to serve a life sentence?

STEVE.

You're right. Five hundred dollars it is. (*Counts on his fingers.*) Five hundred into twenty-five thousand goes fifty— Well, Jim and I are safe for fifty weeks, anyway.

BOWIE.

(*Pompously.*) You will be safe as long as the American flag waves over the consulate.

[35]

STEVE.

And you get the rent.

BOWIE.

(*Looking cautiously about.*) Listen! I have more power in this country than you suppose. What I can't do for you as Consul, I'll do for you—as Dictator. Do you know Pedro Rivas, "El Muerto"?

STEVE.

(*Putting his hand inside his coat.*) Yes, but let me give you one of *my* cigars.

BOWIE.

He's not a cigar—he's a revolutionist. (*Impressively.*) He is known as "El Muerto, a killer, a slayer of men."

STEVE.

(*Offering cigar.*) That's what this is—try it.

BOWIE.

Listen! I am the man back of General Rivas—he is only a uniform, a man of straw. He is my cat's-paw.

STEVE.

Oh!

BOWIE.

Two weeks ago I made him President. From New York I furnished the plans, money, and men. Now I am here to take my reward. In this Republic *I* am the government. My word is law, and you—are under my protection. So, get your things together and join me on shore. And if that detective troubles you again, refer him to the American Consul—and he will face the Dictator of San Manana!

STEVE.

Hurrah! (*He runs to cabin door. Calling into cabin.*) Jim! Jim!

JIM.

(*Appearing at cabin window.*) Yes, sir.

STEVE.

Are my things packed?

JIM.

Yes, sir. Are we going ashore?

STEVE.

I should say we *were* going ashore. (*Impressively.*) I've bought the protection of the Dictator of San Manana.

JIM.

(*Whispering.*) Really, sir. What's a Dictator, sir?

STEVE.

(*In a whisper.*) I don't know, but—(points *at* BOWIE *who is at the rail tearing up the "I. O. U.'s" and throwing them into the water*)—he's one of them and I've bought him. In New York—I think he'd be—a police captain. (*Exits into cabin.* VASQUEZ, *the Health Officer, enters upper left. He is small, excitable, dark-skinned, and with mustache and goatee. He wears a blue drill uniform, with much gold lace, and a Panama hat turned up at one side by a cockade.*)

VASQUEZ.

Hist! Hist! (BOWIE *turns.* VASQUEZ *with one hand makes a sign in the air.*)

BOWIE.

At last! (*He makes the same sign with his right hand.* VASQUEZ *repeats.*) *Viva, Rivas!*

[37]

VASQUEZ.

Viva, Rivas!

BOWIE.

Good!

VASQUEZ.

You are Colonel Bowie, the American Consul?

BOWIE.

Yes.

VASQUEZ.

(*In a cautious whisp*er.) I am Vasquez, the Health Officer—General Rivas sent me to meet you.

BOWIE.

(*Loudly and angrily.*) Well, you go back to General Rivas and tell him to send three generals of the army to meet *me*, not a two-spot Health Officer. (*With increasing anger.*) Tell General Rivas to come here himself.

VASQUEZ.

(*In amazement.*) To come himself? Ah! they have not told you of the revolution.

BOWIE.

(*Scornfully.*) Told me of the revolution? Why, I made the revolution.

VASQUEZ.

Yes, *two weeks* ago, but not *last Tuesday!*

BOWIE.

Last Tuesday!

VASQUEZ.

Last Tuesday General Campos, with five thousand dollars, defeated Rivas in a great battle. Five privates were wounded and twenty-three generals.

BOWIE.

Defeated! And where is Rivas now?

VASQUEZ.

(*Pointing over the rail.*) There!

BOWIE.

Drowned?

VASQUEZ.

No, in the fortress, in the dungeon below the sea wall. The water drips upon him through the stones. And the cell next to his is being kept wet—for you.

BOWIE.

For me?

VASQUEZ.

For you. Campos knows you are the man who sent Rivas against him——

BOWIE.

Well, then, he also knows that I am the American Consul—and he doesn't dare touch me.

VASQUEZ.

Ah! but you are not yet—the American Consul.

BOWIE.

(*Producing official looking envelope.*) There are my credentials to prove it.

VASQUEZ.

But President Campos will not receive them. If you put your foot on that wharf, you are only a private citizen and he will shoot you against the wall. He has promised it—to the people. (BOWIE seizes VASQUEZ *by the throat and shakes him.*)

[39]

BOWIE.

You little devil! I don't believe you! I don't believe you!

VASQUEZ.

You don't believe me! And I have risked my life to tell you! Ah! (*Turns and points toward the city of Porto Banos.*) Look! Do you see in any place the blue flag of Rivas? No, not one! On the palace, on the fortress, on every house in Porto Banos, you see the *yellow* flag of Campos, the yellow flag of *Campos.* (BOWIE *turns and looks at the town, then throws up his arms with a gesture of despair.*)

BOWIE.

The game's up! They've robbed me! They've ruined me! (BOWIE *comes down left. The cabin door opens and* STEVE *backs upon the stage, holding one end of a steamer trunk, while the other end is held by* JIM. *At sight of* VASQUEZ *he drops his end of the trunk. He addresses* BOWIE, *pointing at* VASQUEZ.) Who's he, Steve? Is he all right?

BOWIE.

(*Roughly.*) Yes—he's all right! (*Aside to* VASQUEZ.) Not a word to him.

VASQUEZ.

No, señor. (STEVE *advances, leaving* JIM *in front of cabin.*)

STEVE.

(*Going up to* BOWIE, *cheerfully.*) Well, Colonel, when do we go ashore?

BOWIE.

(*Pacing angrily up and down.*) Never!

STEVE.

(*Keeping* step *with him.*) Never!

BOWIE.

I've changed my mind.

STEVE.

Changed your mind?

BOWIE.

I'm going to Jamaica.

STEVE.

(*Furiously.*) See here, *you* can't change your mind. You can't go to Jamaica. You're not Consul to Jamaica. Who's going to protect *me*? *I* can't go to Jamaica.

BOWIE.

I'm not Consul anywhere until I present these papers, and I don't mean to present them. (*Holds envelope forward.*) I don't want to *die!*

STEVE.

Die!

BOWIE.

(*Slowly, as he formulates his excuse.*) Yes, die! (*Glances warningly at* VASQUEZ.) *I'm* willing to die for my country at my post of duty, but my young bride shall not be sacrificed. This is the Health Officer of the port. He has come out to warn the passengers not to go on shore. He tells us that the town is rotten with yellow fever.

STEVE.

Yellow fever! (*To* VASQUEZ.) Is that true?

BOWIE.

True! Look for yourself! (*Points.*) Every house **in** Porto Banos has a yellow-fever flag.

[41]

STEVE.

Well, what's yellow fever? I'd rather take my chance with yellow fever than be hanged. You can't desert your post. You can't desert me. If it's a question of a few thousand dollars——

BOWIE.

(*Wildly.*) Thousand dollars! It's a question of life and death.

STEVE.

Well, it's a question of life and death with me. *You* can go to Jamaica. But the only place where I'm safe is in that consulate, and the only man who can save me is the American Consul. (BOWIE *gives a sudden start, and turns with great impressiveness to* VASQUEZ.)

BOWIE.

Doctor, my wife is afraid of your yellow fever!

VASQUEZ.

Yes, señor.

BOWIE.

We have been married only a week.

VASQUEZ.

(*Sympathetically.*) Yes, señor.

BOWIE.

But that young man has no wife, and he isn't afraid of yellow fever. Have you ever seen him in Porto Banos?

VASQUEZ.

No, señor.

BOWIE.

Have you ever seen *me* in Porto Banos?

[42]

VASQUEZ.

No, señor.

BOWIE.

Does anybody know me in Porto Banos? (*He scowls threateningly at* VASQUEZ.)

VASQUEZ.

(*Faintly.*) No—o—señor.

BOWIE.

(*Turns to* STEVE *and gives him the Consul's credentials.*) Go to the consulate, where you are safe, and serve your country as Colonel John T. Bowie, American Consul——

STEVE.

(*With delight.*) Do you mean it?

BOWIE.

I do! (*Grandiloquently.*) I give you my high honors— to save a dear friend's life.

STEVE.

(*In brisk, business-like tones, producing bank-note case.*) How much do you charge to save a dear friend's life?

BOWIE.

(*With equal briskness.*) The salary for four years, and fees, would be five thousand dollars.

STEVE.

(*Pointing at* VASQUEZ.) But this man knows.

BOWIE.

He can be fixed.

STEVE.

(*To* VASQUEZ.) *Can* you be fixed?

VASQUEZ.

(*Eagerly.*)   Yes, señor.

STEVE.

But there is General Rivas.

BOWIE.

Why, I made Rivas.   When I met Pedro Rivas he was a waiter in a Mexican restaurant on Twenty-eighth Street. *I* made him President of San Manana.

STEVE.

Good!   I guess I'd better see General Rivas as soon as I'm landed.

BOWIE.

(*Impressively.*)   I can promise you as soon as you're landed—you will see General Rivas.

STEVE.

Good again!   (*Counts money.*)   Bless the bookmakers! (*To* BOWIE, *handing money.*)   There's your graft.   (*To* VASQUEZ, *giving him money.*)   And there's yours.   That leaves me nineteen thousand dollars to start a new life under a new flag, and a new name, as Colonel John T. Bowie, American Consul to Porto Banos.   Jim, I appoint you Vice-Consul.

JIM.

Thank you, Steve.

STEVE.

Not Steve, now—Colonel.

JIM.

Yes, Colonel.   What are the duties of a Vice-Consul?

STEVE.

I don't know the duties of a Consul yet.   We'll go ashore

and find out. (HYNE *enters briskly upper right.* VASQUEZ *is down to right of* BOWIE. HYNE *offers letter to* BOWIE.)

HYNE.

Here's a letter for you, Consul. (BOWIE *hesitates and points to* STEVE. HYNE *turns inquiringly to* STEVE.)

STEVE.

(*Embarrassed.*) Hyne, the Consul has resigned his position as Consul. He's going to Jamaica and I'm— I'm Acting Consul now.

HYNE.

Oh!

STEVE.

Hyne, this steamship line's been using the consulate as an office for its wireless——

HYNE.

Yes, but I'm going to move it right out.

STEVE.

No, don't! Just keep it where it is, and if anything comes over the water—that you think I'd like to know— you might just mention it. My name is Colonel John T. Bowie now, and *your* salary is a hundred dollars a week. (*About to offer bank notes.*)

HYNE.

That's all right! (*Waves away the money.*) I'll call you anything you like. (*Hands letter to* STEVE *and moves up right.*) Our agent brought that on board. It's from a lady at the hotel, Colonel Bowie. (*Goes off behind smoking room.*)

STEVE.

(*Looking at address on envelope.*) At the hotel? (*To.*

Bowie.) You robber. You rascal! You told me *no one* knew you in Porto Banos.

BOWIE.

No one does, I swear to Heaven! I've never been there. I don't know what this means. (*Takes letter and looks at address; starts back in* terror.) Juanita!

STEVE.

Who's he?

BOWIE.

He isn't a he, he's a she. It's a widow from Panama. We were engaged to be married. (*Glances about fear-fully,* sees VASQUEZ, *and moves* STEVE *to centre.*) Don't let my wife know this. (*Sadly.*) It's all up. We can't fix Juanita. (*Reluctantly offers to return the money to* STEVE.)

STEVE.

(*Hopelessly*) No?

BOWIE.

(*Firmly.*) Not—Juanita! Give me back those papers.

STEVE.

(*After consideration.*) I'll take my chances with Juanita.

BOWIE.

You'd better not take any more chances with Juanita than you have to. (*Offers letter.*)

STEVE.

What's she like—Juanita?

BOWIE.

They call her the Star of Panama! (*Fervently.*) She's the most beautiful woman under the Southern Cross!

[46]

STEVE.

Give me that letter. (STEVE *takes letter and reads it aloud.*) "Dearest Jack"— (*To* BOWIE.) She calls me Jack, does she? "I have heard of your appointment as Consul to Porto Banos, and I have crossed the Isthmus to join you. If you do not keep your engagement to marry me——"

BOWIE.

Be careful! Don't let Mrs. Bowie hear you.

STEVE.

What's Mrs. Bowie got to do with this? *She* hasn't promised to marry the girl—*I* have. I'm the one that's got to be careful— (*Reads.*) "If you do not keep your engagement to marry me, I will not sue you for breach of promise, as my sisters of the cold North do." (*Smiles.*) Juanita is rather poetical—"but"— (STEVE, *while in his left hand he holds* JUANITA's *letter—at which he gazes in horror, with his right hand offers to return the credentials to* BOWIE.)

BOWIE.

What is it?

STEVE.

(*Reads.*) "But I shall plant my dagger in your heart." (*Explosively.*) I don't care if Juanita is the most beautiful woman under all the stars! (*He tries to force the credentials upon* BOWIE.)

BOWIE.

(*Backing from* STEVE *and refusing the papers.*) Nonsense! Nonsense! She'll *see* you're not the man who promised to marry her, and you can tell her that you are the real John T. Bowie, and that the first one was an impostor, that I am an impostor—a rascal.

[47]

STEVE.

Yes, I can tell her that. Come on, Jim, who's afraid?
(*Turns to go up* centre. Vasquez *rushes toward him.*)

VASQUEZ.

No, I cannot permit this! (*Offers bank* notes.) Take
back your money. Go to Jamaica. If you go on shore
there—(points *to* Porto *Banos*)—you will surely *die.*

BOWIE.

(*Pushing him back.*) Silence, you idiot!

STEVE.

(*Lightly.*) Oh, thanks! but I'm not afraid of yellow
fever. I rather like this excitement. I'm just beginning
to enjoy myself. (STEVE *turns to upper right as* DUFFY
rushes on from upper left. STEVE *recoils in* terror *upon*
JIM *over trunk and against ladder.*)

DUFFY.

(*Shouting.*) I'm a secret-service detective. (*To* STEVE.)
Would you like to see my badge?

STEVE.

(*Crowding back upon* JIM; *trying to get up ladder, over*
JIM.) No, I don't want to see your badge; I told you I
didn't want to see your badge.

DUFFY.

(*To all.*) The Captain informs me that Colonel Bowie,
the American Consul, is on this ship. Which of you is he?

STEVE.

What do you want with the American Consul?

DUFFY.

(*Turning to* STEVE.) What business is that of yours?

STEVE.

(*Hysterically.*) What business is that of mine? What business? That's funny! Why— Well, why don't you tell him? why don't somebody tell him?

BOWIE.

(*Pointing to* STEVE.) *That* gentleman is the American Consul.

DUFFY.

(*Subserviently.*) Oh, I beg your pardon! I beg your pardon!

STEVE.

That's all right! That's all right! (*Anxiously.*) But don't mistake me for anybody else, though.

DUFFY.

No, sir. I was cabled to come here from Porto Banos to find two men—from New York. Mr. Brooke Travers and valet. (STEVE *and* JIM *collapse against each other.*)

STEVE.

(*Aside to* JIM.) Stand up—stand up—remember you're a Vice-Consul. Act like one.

DUFFY.

They are believed to have sailed for Porto Banos. Now, there are only six Americans in Porto Banos, and one of them I believe to be Brooke Travers, and I have arrested him on suspicion.

STEVE.

(*Eagerly.*) You have arrested him *already*.

DUFFY.

I have him safe in jail! And all I need now, Mr..

Consul, to take him to New York, is your official permission.

STEVE.

(*Wildly.*) My permission? You want *my* permission! You can have my permission, you can have the Vice-Consul's permission, too. You are a great detective, you shall be promoted for this. Next summer you'll be guarding the lawn at Oyster Bay. Come on, Jim! (STEVE *and* JIM *pick up the steamer trunk, and start happily up stage.*)

DUFFY.

(*Saluting.*) Thank you, Colonel. Your good wife— (STEVE *stops suddenly.*) Mrs. Bowie told me you would be sure to help me.

STEVE.

(*Astonished.*) My good wife—Mrs. Bowie? (*Nervously.*) Oh, yes, you've seen her?

DUFFY.

It was she told me I'd find you here.

STEVE.

Well, we won't wait for her now, she can come later. We'll go on shore—we'll go quick (*turns to* BOWIE) and find Rivas—(BOWIE *and* VASQUEZ *exchange glances*)—and start this criminal back to New York. (MRS. BOWIE *enters briskly.*)

DUFFY.

(*Pointing to* STEVE.) Ah, Mrs. Bowie, I've found your husband.

MRS. BOWIE.

(*Staring at* STEVE.) That's not my— (STEVE *clasps her in his arms, and to drown her voice shouts excitedly.*)

[50]

STEVE.

Good-by, Julia, I'm going ashore! Back in just a minute!

MRS. BOWIE.

(*Struggling, calls to her husband.*) John! John! Help me! (LUCY *enters upper left, carrying travelling bags; at sight of* MRS. BOWIE *in the arms of* STEVE *she drops the travelling bags.*)

STEVE.

(*To* MRS. BOWIE.) Don't call me John, call me Jack! Good-by. Good-by! (*He kisses her, and sees* LUCY.) Good heavens! (*Followed by* JIM *he rushes off right as* MRS. BOWIE *falls, shrieking hysterically, into the arms of* BOWIE.)

CURTAIN.

ACT II.

This scene represents the interior of the United States Consulate at Porto Banos. The consulate is situated in a square room built for a hot climate with high ceiling and thick adobe walls, the ceiling resting on cross beams which apparently allow the air to circulate between it and the top of the walls. For five feet from the floor the walls are tinted with a light cobalt blue; above that they are whitewashed. In the centre of the back wall is a high doorway with a curved top. On each side of the doorway is an iron-barred window. In the left wall of the room is a door, which is supposed to open in the ante-room of the consulate, which leads to the street. From the stage this door is reached by two wooden steps, the sill of the door making a third step. On the wall below the door hangs a large, much-stained school map of the United States. In the right wall, far up, is a door opening into what is supposed to be the Consul's bedroom. Below the door is the Consul's flat desk. Below that against the wall a bentwood rocking chair. In front of the desk is a swivel or office chair and a Mexican waste-paper basket. On the desk are official-looking papers, State Department reports in red-linen covers, and a stamp for sealing papers, such as are used by notaries public. Under the left window on a table are the Leyden jars and apparatus of the wireless telegraph. It has the appearance of an ordinary Morse receiver. From it wires run out of the left window. This room is supposed to be in one wing of the Hotel del Prado, which is built around a garden, or patio, and it is situated on a cliff overlooking the harbor. The fourth side of the garden, the side which is not surrounded by the hotel, is open upon the cliff where there is a narrow street. Looking through the windows and door in the back wall the audience sees on the back drop the hotel garden, and directly across it the other wing of the hotel. Through the right window they see the main building of the hotel. Through the left window is visible the ocean over the edge of the cliff and the ships at anchor in the harbor. In front of the back drop is a practical flagpole, with its top disappearing above the centre door. When the flag is hoisted on this pole its folds hang just in view. An American flag tied in a roll hangs from the halyards, which are tied to a cleat. In front of the flagpole, and running from left to right, is a row of tropical plants in green wooden tubs. Between these and the centre wall of the consulate a path is supposed to run toward the right to the main part of the hotel.

At rise of Curtain HYNE is discovered at the wireless table receiving and sending messages. There is much ticking of the instrument, and flashes and sputterings from the electric lights. JOSÉ, the landlord, a bejewelled and excitable Spanish-American, enters through the centre door. He is followed by a SERVANT carrying two framed portraits, one of George Washington and one of General Jackson. Another servant follows, balancing on his head a tin bath tub in which is set a tin water pitcher. Over his left arm are a number of bath towels.

HYNE.

Hello, José! Is the Consul over at your hotel?

JOSÉ.

(*Bustles up to* HYNE.) Ah, my good friend, I am glad⸱ No, the Consul has not arrived. I prepare for him. I am ver'—busy—ver'—busy. He comes now—ver'—soon. (*To* SERVANT.) Pron*to!* Pron*to!* (*He takes a portrait from the servant and waves the other servant impatiently to the door of the bedroom.*) *Por aqui, por aqui.* (*With bath tub the* SERVANT *exits right.* JOSÉ *steps upon the chair and then to the desk, and hangs picture on a nail in the wall, bustling actively.*)

HYNE.

Look out! don't break your neck! You've plenty of time! The Consul was still on the ship when I left. I've just sent a wireless to our second mate to find out where he is. (JOSÉ *takes second picture from* SERVANT *and hangs it next to the other.* SERVANT *reënters from room, and exits with other servant.*)

JOSÉ.

(*On desk.*) What do you want with the Consul, hey?

HYNE.

Oh! Campos, this new President of yours, he's held up our ship till the Consul signs her papers.

JOSÉ.

Ah, I suspect the new President wants—a little fee. (*Coming down from desk.*)

HYNE.

Your presidents would starve if they couldn't rob our steamship line. (*Key of wireless sounds.*)

[54]

JOSÉ

Your talking machine, it talks all right, now, hey? (HYNE, *apparently listening to message, nods.*) Who you talk to now? (*He passes into the garden at centre and unwinds flag from flagpole.*)

HYNE.

Talking to the ship. Second officer says (*listens*) "The old man's howling for his papers." (*Takes bundle of papers from his pocket and crossing to desk places them upon it.*)

JOSÉ.

(*Having hoisted the flag.*) That is good. It is six— seven months since a Consul put up that flag.

HYNE.

Yes, and then he put it at half mast for the last Consul that died— (*Looks at portraits over desk.*) Are those yours?

JOSÉ.

(*Coming down to left.*) No, not mine. What good are they in the consulate when there is no Consul? So I have hang them in my barroom. It makes the Americans in Puerto Banos feel just like home.

HYNE.

Which—the pictures or the barroom? I guess I'll go over and see if I can't feel at home. Tell Colonel Bowie to be careful *whose name* he signs to those papers.

JOSÉ.

What is that?

HYNE.

(*Takes up papers and then at centre door turns back.*) Never mind, I'll do it myself. Oh, José, tell me something.

Tell me the truth. But break it to me gently. *Is* the ice machine out of order this morning?

JOSÉ.

No, señor.

HYNE.

Saved! Saved! (*Exit.*)

(*The voice of* DUFFY *is heard off left.*) 'Tention! Right face! March! (*A native policeman enters left.*) Halt! (DUFFY *enters with the* REV. MR. BOSTICK, *followed by another policeman.* DUFFY *and* BOSTICK *are handcuffed together.* BOSTICK *has a ball and chain attached to his left ankle. He is a well-built, serious-looking young man, in a much-soiled white flannel shirt and trousers, black alpaca coat, and black straw hat. Wisps of straw stick in his flannels, and he wears a knotted handkerchief instead of a collar. At ordinary times he would be smooth-shaven, but now he has a week's growth of beard, which gives him a disreputable appearance. He speaks in a peevish, angry manner.*)

JOSÉ.

(*Coming down quickly.*) That man must not come in here. (*Points to* BOSTICK.)

DUFFY.

Why not? You know me—Duffy—secret-service detective.

JOSÉ.

(*Impatiently.*) Yes, I know you, I know you! What you want?

DUFFY.

I want the Consul.

BOSTICK.

(*Defiantly.*) Yes, and *I* want the Consul. Where is the American Consul?

DUFFY.

Don't you worry, young man; you've been howling to see the Consul, and now you're going to see him. (*To* José.) Where's Colonel Bowie?

JOSÉ.

(*Crossing right toward door to anteroom.*) I go look out for him now.

DUFFY.

We'll wait here.

JOSÉ.

(*Jeeringly.*) You got prisoner at last, hey? I'm glad. I'm afraid you take me. That man he can't stop here. Put him into the patio. (*Goes out left.*)

DUFFY.

(*Calling after him.*) Tell the Consul we'll wait for him in the hotel. (*He starts toward the centre door. By means of the handcuff* BOSTICK *drags* DUFFY *back.*)

BOSTICK.

I demand that these irons be taken off my wrist.

DUFFY.

There you go again—always thinking of yourself. Can't you see I have to wear 'em too?

BOSTICK.

You wait till the Board of Missions learns of this.

DUFFY.

Oh, cut out the Board of Missions! You're a nice looking missionary!

BOSTICK.

I admit that after a week in a dungeon my appearance is

against me. But I *am* a missionary—the Rev. Arthur Bostick.

DUFFY.

Well, if you're the Rev. Arthur Bostick, why did you tell me your name was Jim Robinson?

BOSTICK.

(*In distress.*) I don't know. I did it when I was frightened. The disgrace, the indignity of being arrested, I, a clergyman, arrested as a criminal! And I was expecting a friend on this steamer. I didn't want her to know. I don't want her to know now. I admit it was wrong of me. It was a lie.

DUFFY.

(*Cheerfully.*) I know it was a lie. Your name is Brooke Travers.

BOSTICK.

I tell you my name is Arthur Bostick.

DUFFY.

Well, prove it.

BOSTICK.

How can I prove it here; no one knows me here. I tell you, I came in from the Pacific side. But back there in the mountains everybody knows me. (*Appealingly.*) It's only a six days' ride.

DUFFY.

Yes, I see myself riding into these mountains alone with you. You'd lead me into an ambush and escape. I've caught you in one plot to escape.

BOSTICK.

I—tried to escape? Now, see here, you, if you dare—

DUFFY.

(*Pulling* BOSTICK'S *hand down by means of the hand-cuff.*) Don't you raise your hand to me. You did plot to escape last night, and (*touching* pocket) I have a warrant here for your—accomplice.

BOSTICK.

Bah! I have no accomplice.

DUFFY.

Who's been bringing food to the jail for you this last week?

BOSTICK.

Well, *you* haven't.

DUFFY.

Well, who has?

BOSTICK.

A very honorable, charitable lady.

DUFFY.

Yes, your accomplice.

BOSTICK.

You idiot! Why, I never saw the lady until I was in jail. She came there with the Governor out of curiosity, and when she found a clergyman locked in with brigands and murderers, and starving, yes, starving—her heart was touched——

DUFFY.

It was! I read her letters.

BOSTICK.

You read her letters—to me?

DUFFY.

There was one in each basket of food, and they were the *love* letters of an accomplice.

BOSTICK.

They were letters of sympathy from a noble-hearted woman. I—I admit Juanita's style is rather tropical, even passionate——

DUFFY.

I know all about Juanita, and I'll tell you what else I know. Yesterday you didn't get anything to eat.

BOSTICK.

(*Savagely.*) I know that just as well as you do!

DUFFY.

(*Triumphantly.*) And why? Because I captured yesterday's basket of food, and the letter in it—and I stopped your plot to escape.

BOSTICK.

There was no plot to escape.

DUFFY.

Oh, no! She only plotted to "fly with her beloved to this mountain home."

BOSTICK.

(*Excitedly.*) Fly with me—"her beloved"?—Juanita proposed— (*Feeling the stubble on his chin.*) Look here, Duffy—before I see Juan—before I see the Consul, can't I make myself a little cleaner? If he sees me like this, he'll never believe I'm a missionary.

DUFFY.

You certainly are a shine-looking missionary.

BOSTICK.

Just a shave and a bath—or—or, just a collar, even?

[60]

THE DICTATOR

DUFFY.

Yes, that's fair! Well, you'll have to hurry. We got to take that steamer inside of one hour, soon as the Consul signs your extradition paper. You'll have time for a shave and a collar—but— (*Looks at handcuffs.*) I don't see how you can take a bath without my taking one too, and I won't do that. I won't do it! (*He calls off left to* JOSÉ.) Hello there, José!

JOSÉ.

(*Speaking from the* anteroom.) Well.

DUFFY.

We're going to the hotel—to find the barber. The moment the Consul gets here—let me know. (JOSÉ *appears in doorway.*)

JOSÉ.

Yes, I'll tell him.

DUFFY.

Don't forget! (*They exit at* centre. José *walks to* centre *and* stands *looking after them.* *A* porter *enters* left, *carrying a* steamer *trunk.*)

JOSÉ.

Que esta ?

PORTER.

El consolato Americano!

JOSÉ.

(*Joyfully.*) Ah, the Consul! (*Waves* PORTER *to room,* left.) *Por aqui, por qui!* (PORTER *carries trunk to door of bedroom and exits. José runs to door left and speaks off, bowing low.*) Good morning, Excellency. I make you welcome, Excellency! (STEVE *and* JIM *enter from the anteroom.*)

STEVE.

Good morning! How do you do? Who are *you*? (PORTER *returning from room right, after placing trunk, and disappears* centre.)

JOSÉ.

I am José, the landlord! This is my hotel. It is yours.

STEVE.

Thank you very much. We're looking for the consulate.

JOSÉ.

This is the consulate. It is yours.

STEVE.

Thank you, again.

JOSÉ.

(*Pointing.*) And this is the sleeping room of the Consul —and there is my hotel, where you come for *la comida*— the food—to eat. And there is the telegraph—the wireless.

STEVE.

Wireless? (*Points to door, left.*) And in there—is that mine, too?

JOSÉ.

Yes, Excellency, the room on the street is for the Vice-Consul.

STEVE.

(*To* JIM.) You have a room on the street. What's the name of that street?

JOSÉ.

It is called Bogran, in memory of the great President Bogran. He was President long, long time—eight months.

STEVE.

You mean years?

JOSÉ.

No! Eight months is long time to be President in San Manana. Bogran was *good* President. He was assassinated.

STEVE.

Assassinated? (*To* JIM, *right.*) I wonder what they do to a *bad* President? Then all this wing of the hotel is the consulate?

JOSÉ.

Si, señor, for ten years. Since I keep the hotel I know three, four, five Consuls!

STEVE.

Indeed!

JOSÉ.

(*Sadly.*) All die.

STEVE.

All what?

JOSÉ.

All die.

JIM.

(*Timidly.*) What—what did they die of?

JOSÉ.

Just the fever.

JIM.

Fever!

STEVE.

And are *we* likely to die of fever, too?

JOSÉ.

No, no! I take good care of you. Fever not touch you if you come my hotel and I give you big glass brandy.

[63]

STEVE.

Why didn't the other Consuls take "big glass brandy"?

JOSÉ.

(*Indignantly.*)   They take too many glass brandy.

STEVE.

(*To* JIM.)   We lose both ways.   (*He sinks despondently into the swivel chair.*)   And I was so anxious to get this job that I paid five thousand dollars for it.   Jolly place this to spend the rest of your life in.   Only comfort I can see is that it will be short life.   (*Picks up stamp on desk.*)   Is this the consular seal?

JOSÉ.

Yes, Excellency.   I—myself—prepared everything for you as soon as I received your letter.

STEVE.

(*Startled.*)   My letter?   (JIM *nudges him.*)   Oh, yes, so I wrote you I was coming, did I?

JOSÉ.

Yes, Consul, but you wrote me also that madame, your wife, was coming.

STEVE.

(*Rises.*)   My wife!   (*Turns to* JIM.)

JOSÉ.

She is not coming, no?

STEVE.

My wife, no, no, she's not coming!   No!   You see the Health Officer told us about the fever, so I sent her on to Jamaica.   (*Fiercely.*)   And she'll stay in Jamaica until I send for her.

JOSÉ.

Ah, I am sorry!

STEVE.

Yes, I'm sorry too. I'll miss—I'll miss— (*Aside to* JIM.) What's the name of my wife?

JIM.

Julia.

STEVE.

Julia. (*To* JOSÉ.) Yes, I'll miss Julia very much, dear little Julia, bless her!

JOSÉ.

(*Mysteriously.*) Perhaps, Excellency, it is just so good that she did not come.

STEVE.

What's that?

JOSÉ.

Pardon, Excellency, but perhaps it is just as good as she did not come until the *other* lady has gone away.

STEVE.

Other lady? What other lady?

JOSÉ.

The lady in my hotel—who is waiting to marry you.

STEVE.

Waiting to marry me! (*To* JIM.) Juanita! (*To* JOSÉ.) Is *she* in this hotel? I mean, is there a woman in this hotel who says *I'm* going to marry her? She must be mad! What nonsense! Why, I *am* married—married to Edna!

JIM.

(*In a quick whisper.*) Julia!

[65]

STEVE.

Yes, Julia, dear little Julia—down in Jamaica!

JOSÉ.

I am sorry, Excellency! The señora tells my wife you come here to marry her, but when I read the Excellency's letter and he says his wife comes with him—I tell my wife to say nothing.

STEVE.

That's quite right! Don't let that woman know I'm here.

JOSÉ.

But she saw the ship come in.

STEVE.

Well, she can see the ship, but she mustn't see me. Before I see anybody I must pay my respects to the President. I haven't presented my credentials yet. (*He takes credentials from pocket and shows a loose page.*) And there's my speech. I don't know a word of it. I hope the President will like my speech. Bowie wrote it. Jim, old man, would you mind opening my trunk and laying out my frock coat and high hat?

JIM.

High hat, sir?

STEVE.

Yes—in the tropics I have noticed that diplomats and American dentists always wear silk hats.

JIM.

Certainly! (*Exit left.*)

STEVE.

Now listen, landlord! There is a secret-service detective——

JOSÉ.

Señor Duffy?

STEVE.

Oh, you know him?

JOSÉ.

(*Indignantly.*) We *all* know him! He has tried to arrest everybody!

STEVE.

That's the man. Well, he has arrested some one at last, and I'm going to ship him and his prisoner on that steamer (points *off upper left*) to New York by way of Jamaica. He's gone to the jail——

JOSÉ.

No, Excellency, he is at my hotel.

STEVE.

(*Eagerly.*) Has he got a prisoner with him?

JOSÉ.

Yes, Excellency!

STEVE.

(*Delightedly.*) Good! Tell him I want to see him. (JOSÉ *turns up and looks off left.*)

JOSÉ.

Si, señor. Ah! a lady, Excellency.

STEVE.

(*Terrified.*) A lady! I'm not at home! I'm out! Is it *that* lady?

JOSÉ.

No, señor. (LUCY *appears in door left.*)

[67]

STEVE.

Ah, Miss Sheridan! Ah, do come in! (LUCY *coldly* turns *her head from him and addresses* JOSÉ.)

LUCY.

Is this the United States Consulate?

JOSÉ.

Si, señorita.

LUCY.

Colonel Bowie, the Consul, has he arrived?

JOSÉ.

Si, señorita. This gentleman——

STEVE.

(*Waving him off left.*) That'll do, landlord; that'll do. (*Crosses to* JOSÉ, *and pushes him up* steps.) The lady knows who I am perfectly well. You don't have to tell her who *I* am. Just wait in there please, and when I'm ready for the detective, I'll ask you to bring him here.

JOSÉ.

Si, señor. (*Exit left.*)

STEVE.

(*Cordially turning to* LUCY.) My! It is good to see you again. I was afraid——

LUCY.

Pardon me, but I am here to see the Consul——

STEVE.

The Consul—yes—but while he—eh—while we're waiting for the Consul have you any objections to my company?

LUCY.

I have—very strong objections.

STEVE.

I beg your pardon.

LUCY.

As any woman would—after your conduct.

STEVE.

My—conduct? When?

LUCY.

You know when.

STEVE.

(*After a pause.*) Oh!

LUCY.

Yes.

STEVE.

You mean when I left the ship—Mrs. Bowie— (*With disgust.*) Julia!

LUCY.

(*Indignantly.*) Julia!

STEVE.

Yes, wasn't that perfectly outrageous?

LUCY.

It *was*!

STEVE.

I was never so embarrassed in my life—to be suddenly embraced—by a married woman——

LUCY.

(*Coldly.*) I didn't see that.

STEVE.

Didn't you see that? Oh, it was awful! Oh! you ought to have seen that. If you didn't—*see* it, you wouldn't believe it.

LUCY.

I *don't* believe it? I saw—*you*—force your attentions upon a lady against her protest, in spite of her struggles.

STEVE.

(*In a tone of indignation.*) Well, well, well! Now, that shows you no one is safe, no one is safe. If *you* could turn things against me that way, no innocent man is safe.

LUCY.

But I saw you—and the passengers saw you—and her husband saw you.

STEVE.

(*Triumphantly.*) Ah! You admit her husband saw me—and yet—and yet—you never guessed!

LUCY.

(*Turning away from him.*) I never guessed you cared for Mrs. Bowie!

STEVE.

I—care for Mrs. Bowie! You—say that to—me! I merely—it was this way—I will explain how it happened— (*She moves away impatiently.*) No, I insist—you have doubted me, and I will explain. And I'm going to tell the truth, too.

LUCY.

Of course you are.

STEVE.

Of course I am. Mrs. Bowie was er—er—thanking me.

[70]

LUCY.

Thanking you?

STEVE.

That was all. Thanking me. She was grateful. I had rendered her husband a slight service. You know there's yellow fever here?

LUCY.

Well?

STEVE.

Well, it's very bad, and they wanted to go to Jamaica and wait there until the fever here was stamped out, but they couldn't go to Jamaica because he had no money.

LUCY.

Why not?

STEVE.

Because he lost it all to me on his way down—betting on the run. I gave him a run for his money. He got the run, I got the money.

LUCY.

That—was gambling.

STEVE.

Yes, but wait! When I learned I was forcing that young couple to spend their honeymoon in this—fever swamp, I gave him back his money and she, in a burst of gratitude. in her innocent girlish way—threw her arms around my neck, and you—came out at that exact moment and imagined that I—that I— (*His voice breaks with emotion.*) Oh, how could you——

LUCY.

I am very sorry. I didn't know. Won't you—forgive me? (*She comes toward him.*)

STEVE.

(*Magnanimously.*) Of course I will forgive you. But

[71]

how could you doubt me, I—I who have never looked into a woman's eyes until I looked into yours——

LUCY.

(*Moving away*.)   Oh!   You know you must not speak so to me.   I told you not to do it.

STEVE.

Then you mustn't let me see you.   For when I see you, I——

LUCY.

Oh!

STEVE.

"Oh" what?

LUCY.

If Mrs. Bowie has gone to Jamaica, what am *I* to do? Who's to chaperone me?   The Board of Missions put me in charge of the Consul—and his wife?

STEVE.

By Jove! that's so.   But there's Bostick, confound him! By the way, where *is* Bostick?

LUCY.

I—I don't know.

STEVE.

Don't know!   Didn't he meet you?

LUCY.

No.

STEVE.

He didn't!   Hurrah!   Perhaps he's dead!   But he sent some one to meet you.

LUCY.

No.

STEVE.

(*Indignantly.*)   He didn't?

LUCY.

(*Apologetically.*)   He lives very far back in the mountains, six days' ride from the coast, and they tell me the rivers are swollen and the trail is impassable——

STEVE.

(*Fiercely.*)   I'd like to see the swollen river that could keep *me* back if you were coming to marry me!   Why, he should have been camping out at the end of that wharf a month ago, with a telescope stuck in each eye!   I'd like to be on the bank of a swollen river while Bostick was trying to climb the bank.   (*He kicks violently in front of him.*)

LUCY.

You forget yourself!   You are speaking of the man I am going to marry.

STEVE.

I can't help it, if you are going to marry him.   I wish I *could* help it.   Why are you going to marry him, anyway? Because you love him?

LUCY.

Because I have promised to marry him.   I have promised all of them.

STEVE.

(*Violently.*)   *All* of them!   How many more are there?

LUCY.

All of the Board of Missions.   I promised them I would help him in his work.

[73]

STEVE.

How can you help him when he isn't here? Now listen! Bostick has lost his chance. Why don't you give me a chance now? I wish the Board of Missions had put you in charge of me, instead of Bowie.

LUCY.

Yes, but you see Colonel Bowie is our—Consul, and he—has a wife, and you are not the Consul! And you are not married, are you?

STEVE.

(*Thoughtfully.*) No, I suppose not. No, in a way I'm not.

LUCY.

(*Sharply.*) *Are* you married?

STEVE.

How dare you ask me that? I—I who have never looked into a woman's eyes until I looked into yours.

LUCY.

I told you not to say that to me.

STEVE.

Well, then, don't bring your eyes where I am. (JOSÉ *appears excitedly at door left.*)

JOSÉ.

Excellency! Excellency! (JOSÉ *signals in pantomime that there is some one in the room behind him.*)

STEVE.

Who! What!

JOSÉ.

The lady! The widow lady!

STEVE.

Juanita?

JOSÉ.

Si, señor.

STEVE.

(*Running to* LUCY.) Don't desert me! Don't leave me! There's an awful woman coming here, old friend of Bowie's. Bowie, no, I guess you'll have to go. It's a private affair—of Bowie's—Bowie wouldn't like it known.

LUCY.

Of course I'll go. (*Sadly.*) But where?

STEVE.

Where? To the hotel. There's no other place. José, your wife will take care of Miss Sheridan, won't she?

JOSÉ.

(*To* LUCY.) Ah! *si*, señorita. (*Exits into room left.*)

STEVE.

His wife will take care of you. (*He calls.*) Jim! Jim! go with Miss Sheridan to the hotel. (JIM *enters*, JIM *bows, and with* LUCY *moves to door* centre.)

STEVE.

(*Taking* LUCY's *hand and speaking hysterically.*) Good-by, good-by, and if we should never meet again——

LUCY.

Aren't you coming to lunch?

STEVE.

(*Wildly.*) Lunch! In this country you can't look as far into the future as lunch. What with assassinations, revolutions, yellow fever—and— and — Juanita — you're lucky to live till after breakfast. Farewell— (*Taking her hand.*) Remember, I—never looked into a woman's eyes——

LUCY.

(*Indignantly, withdrawing her hand.*) Good morning. (*Exits centre, with* JIM.)

STEVE.

(*Reproachfully.*) Not good morning, good-by, perhaps forever! (JOSÉ *appears at door left.*)

JOSÉ.

Excellency! she will not wait. She is coming. (STEVE *comes down to* JOSÉ.)

STEVE.

(*Desperately.*) Let her come! José, we who are about to die, salute thee. (*He crosses and stands by swivel chair.*)

JOSÉ.

(*Sympathetically.*) Ah, señor! (*Speaks into door left.*) Enter Señora. (JUANITA, *a dark, Spanish-looking woman, enters. She wears a black-lace walking dress, open at the throat ; in her hair is a high comb on which is draped a man-tilla ; she carries a fan. She rushes down steps ; on seeing* STEVE *halts, looks at him, and then turns upon* JOSÉ.)

JUANITA.

(*Looking from* STEVE *to* JOSÉ.) I told you to bring me to Colonel John T. Bowie.

JOSÉ.

Si, señora. (Points *at* STEVE.)

STEVE.

(*Hurriedly.*) That'll do, José. You can—go!

JOSÉ.

I—go, señor. (*Exit eagerly left.*)

JUANITA.

(*Calling after him.*) José! José! (*Turns to* STEVE.)
How dare *you* give commands? That man deceived me.
He told me I would find here Colonel John T. Bowie. (*As
she speaks the name, she stabs the air with her fan as though
it were a dagger.* STEVE *observes this with horrified interest and moves down nearer to table.*)

STEVE.

(*Hesitatingly.*) *I* am Colonel John T. Bowie!

JUANITA.

You! (*Turns away in anger.*) You are crazy!

STEVE.

Yes, I'm nearly crazy; but it is also true, madam, that
I am the Consul.

JUANITA.

Bah! Is this a joke?

STEVE.

(*Hysterically.*) A joke! Hah, hah, I like that! (*Laughs.*)

JUANITA.

(*Fiercely.*) You laugh! (*Moves toward him.*)

STEVE.

(*Retreats to desk.*) I assure you that being Colonel
Bowie—is no joke. (*Takes credentials from table.*) If you
doubt my word, madam, here are my credentials from
the State Department.

JUANITA.

And do you think you are man enough to carry that off?.

STEVE.

(*Smiling ingratiatingly and weighing envelope in his hand.*) That's not heavy!

JUANITA.

Bah! Don't trifle with me! What are you trying to do here? What's your little game, eh?

STEVE.

(*With attempt at dignity.*) My—"game"—madam! I beg you to remember that you are addressing the American Consul—John Bowie! (*He strikes an attitude, and attempts to lean upon the back of the swivel chair, which sinks beneath his weight. He recovers and, folding his arms, scowls fiercely.*)

JUANITA.

You cannot persuade *me* that you are Colonel Bowie. I—who for three years have loved John Bowie; I—who for three years have hated John Bowie!

STEVE.

How are you feeling toward John this morning?

JUANITA.

I hate him so that if I thought you *were* he (*draws dagger from left sleeve*) I would plant this in your treacherous heart.

STEVE.

(*Drawing chair between them.*) But you don't think I'm he. You just said so. I heard you. (Points.) You were standing right over there. The man you want to stab is an impostor.

JUANITA.

You are the impostor! I have known John Bowie in

Panama for eleven years. I would have married him, but my husband objected. When my husband died, Bowie married a Northern woman. Two weeks ago he sailed for this place in that steamer; but to-day, when he read the letter I sent on board, he was afraid to come on shore; and now you—aha! I see—I see—how much did Bowie pay you for this?

STEVE.

Pay me? Oh, yes! I'm making my fortune at this. The Bank of England couldn't pay me for what I'm going through.

JUANITA.

Ah! he did *not* pay you. Then, why do you pretend—unless— (*Triumphantly.*) Ah! I see, I see! (*Eagerly.*) There is a detective here, searching for two Americans from New York. He has arrested a good and noble gentleman, who has lived here for months. If Duffy were not the fool he is, he would know that the only steamer on which these men could have escaped from New York arrived here this morning, and that one passenger, with his friend, came ashore under a name—that is not his. (*She approaches* STEVE, *smiling mockingly, and leans on the chair.*) Tell me, which are you—the valet or Mr. Brooke Travers?

STEVE.

Tell *you*! Madam, compared to you Sherlock Holmes is in the same class with Duffy.

JUANITA.

Don't interrupt me! I'm thinking! You are not the valet. You are the sort of person who would *need* a valet. So *you* are Brooke Travers.

STEVE. `

(*With an attempt at gayety.*) Oh! so I'm Travers, am I?.

[79]

JUANITA.

You know you are.   Now, if I tell Duffy that you're the man he really wants, he will release his prisoner and take *you* back to New York. (*Pause.*)   No, I've nothing against you.   No, I will not send you back to New York.

STEVE.

Oh, well! just arrange this to suit yourself.

JUANITA.

I mean to.   In a few minutes the detective will be here with his prisoner.   He will ask you to sign the extradition paper.   You will refuse to do so and you will set the prisoner free.

STEVE.

Now see here, madam, here is where the worm turns. *I* am running this consulate, and I will *not* set that prisoner free, but I am going to ship him and that damned detective out of this town as fast as that steamer can carry them.

JUANITA.

You are mad!   The prisoner—is the man—I love!   And if you, as the American Consul, do not set him free I will tell Duffy who you are!   Now, if you wish to remain here in peace and safety as John Bowie, the Consul, you will tear up that extradition paper.   If you refuse, Mr. Brooke Travers, you will go back to New York—a prisoner yourself.   Choose!

STEVE.

Choose?   You haven't left me any "choose."   I've *got* to let him go free.

JUANITA.

Ah! I thank you, Consul.

STEVE.

Don't thank me. You drive a hard bargain, madam.

JUANITA.

It is for the man I love. But I can be generous, too. I will help you. Do you believe me? (*She holds out her hand, in the palm of which is the dagger with the blade pointed up her arm.* STEVE *starts to take her hand, sees the dagger, and jumps back.*)

STEVE.

(*Anxiously.*) Aren't you afraid you'll cut yourself?

JUANITA.

Ah, no! I am used to that dagger. And I have used it, too.

STEVE.

Yes, you told me you were a widow. (*A bugle sound off left.* José *enters excitedly.*)

JOSÉ.

Excellency! *El* Presidente! The President. He come to call upon your Excellency.

STEVE.

The President? I say, that's very polite of him, isn't it? How do I look? I ought to have a high hat, José—has he got on a high hat? (*From off left comes the sound of muskets brought to a "ground arms," and a bugle sounds.* JUANITA *starts left.*)

STEVE.

Don't go! I can't speak a word of Spanish; stay here and interpret for me. (JUANITA *returns and stands below table.*) José, run to the hotel and get some champagne, quick! (José *runs off centre.* STEVE *addresses por-*

[81]

traits *on the wall.*) O General Washington and General Jackson, don't look so ashamed of this American Consul; he's doing the best he can. Wait till you hear my speech. (*He runs into bedroom. Bugle and drum sound, and shouts of "Viva el Presidente!"* COLONEL GARCIA *enters and stands at foot of steps.*)

GARCIA.

El Presidente! (*Voices cry, outside, "Viva el Presidente! Viva, viva!" The flare of bugles is repeated.* CAMPOS *enters, accompanied by* CORPORAL, *and soldiers who fall to right and left of steps.* CAMPOS *is a large, fierce-looking man, of dark complexion, in the uniform of a general.*)

CAMPOS.

Where is this Colonel John T. Bowie? (*He sees* JUAN-ITA.) Ah, señora! (*He bows.*)

JUANITA.

(*Making a deep courtesy.*) *El* Presidente! (STEVE *enters from bedroom. He has changed into a frock coat and carries a high hat.*)

CAMPOS.

You are Colonel John T. Bowie——

STEVE.

Yes, your Excellency, I have that honor. (*Reaches behind him for the written copy of his speech, which is lying open on the table, and moves the paper where he can see it. Reading.*) I welcome your Excellency. (*Glances again at speech on desk.*) I mean, "Thank you for *your* welcome, and allow me the honor of presenting my credentials— (*picking up credentials*)—and also to present you with assurances of my distinguished consideration, and the hope that those cordial relations——"

[82]

CAMPOS.

Silence!

STEVE.

I—I beg your pardon!

CAMPOS.

Silence! I will not receive your papers. I will not receive—you! You are under arrest!

STEVE.

Under arrest! (*To* JUANITA.) What's the matter? Doesn't he like my speech?

CAMPOS.

You are under arrest for plotting against me.

STEVE.

(*Indignantly.*) I—plot against you? Why—I made you! I—oh! I see. (*Crosses and takes* CAMPOS *familiarly by the arm.*) Look here, General, can I speak to you alone? Why, I am the last man—my dear General Rivas——

CAMPOS.

(*Savagely withdrawing his arm.*) Rivas!

JUANITA.

(*In a whisper to* STEVE.) That—is not Rivas.

STEVE.

(*Lightly.*) Not Rivas? Oh, I beg your pardon! I thought you were the President. (*Laughs.*)

CAMPOS.

I am the President—by the voice of the people¡

STEVE.

Well, then, by the voice of the people, if you are President, where is Rivas?

CAMPOS.

In jail, waiting to be shotted! (*He turns his back, and whispers with* COLONEL GARCIA.)

STEVE.

(*To* JUANITA.)   Rivas—in jail?

JUANITA.

This is Campos—there has been a revolution.

STEVE.

When?

JUANITA.

Last Tuesday.

STEVE.

Last Tuesday! When we were at sea! Oh! John Bowie! (*To* JUANITA.) *He* knew of this—this is why he wouldn't come on shore. He wasn't afraid of yellow fever. He wasn't even afraid of *you*. It was this he was afraid of. (*Raises his clenched fists in the air.*) O John Bowie, if we ever meet again.

CAMPOS.

Listen to me! I sent my soldiers to the wharf to arrest you, but they did not recognize you by the description. If any of my men had caught you in the street, they would have shotted you against a wall. But here, in the consulate—I cannot touch you.

STEVE.

I'm sorry you're disappointed.

[84]

CAMPOS.

But I will keep you here a prisoner as long as you live.

STEVE.

Keep me a prisoner! My government will send a war-ship down here, and——

CAMPOS.

That! (*Snaps his fingers.*) That—for your government. Before a warship comes to Puerto Banos, you will be dead. You are my prisoner in this room. You will never leave it again. (STEVE *runs to centre door.*) Halt! (*To the* soldiers.) Guard those doors. Do not let that man escape. (*Two soldiers mount guard on either side of the* steps. *Two others go up centre and stand at either side of the doorway. To* STEVE.) If you walk into the patio, you will be shotted. If you go into the street, you will be shotted. Do I speak the English—very plain?

STEVE.

I understand every word you say. But you don't understand me. (*To* JUANITA.) I think this has gone quite far enough. (*To* CAMPOS.) General, you must know that you are the victim of a mistake——

CAMPOS.

Bah! (*He turns to* GARCIA.)

JUANITA.

(*Angrily.*) What are you going to do?

STEVE.

Going to tell him I'm not Colonel Bowie. I don't intend to get "shotted."

[85]

JUANITA.

You cannot do that—I *forbid* it!

STEVE.

Why can't I do it?

JUANITA.

Because—if you are not John Bowie, the Consul, you cannot free the man I love.

STEVE.

Oh, the man you love be hanged! I'm a prisoner myself, now. I've got to get *myself* free.

JUANITA.

No! First free the man I love, and then when we have escaped to the mountains—then let them know that you are not John Bowie.

STEVE.

We! Are—*you* going with him?

JUANITA.

Of course I am.

STEVE.

Hurrah! I'll set him free. (*He turns to* CAMPOS. JOSÉ *enters centre bearing a tray on which are champagne bottles, and glasses filled with champagne.* JIM *and* HYNE, *much excited, follow* JOSÉ.) Now, then, General; sorry to lose you, but if you are quite ready to go— (*To* JOSÉ, *who is approaching* CAMPOS *with champagne.*) No, no! Not for that man—that's the wrong President. (JOSÉ *places champagne on desk.*)

JOSÉ.

(*As he passes* STEVE.) Pardon, Excellency, the detective and the prisoner insist on coming in.

STEVE.

Bring them here at once. (José *exits centre.*) Now, General, this is *my* consulate, and this is my busy day.

CAMPOS.

Bah! (*To* JUANITA.) *A dios, señora.*

JUANITA.

A dios, el Presidente.

CAMPOS.

Good morning, Colonel Bowie.

STEVE.

Drop in whenever you're passing. (*Glancing at soldiers.*) I'm sure to be at home. (CAMPOS *exits with officer left.* DUFFY *and* BOSTICK *enter centre, followed by two policemen.*)

DUFFY.

Ah, Mr. Consul, glad you've arrived. I'm in a great hurry to catch the steamer. Put your seal on this, please. (*Gives extradition paper to* STEVE.) Extradition paper for the prisoner. (JUANITA *draws near to* STEVE *and shows him the dagger.*)

JUANITA.

Remember!

STEVE.

Don't do that! Do you think I'm likely to forget? (*To* DUFFY.) Now, Duffy, you're—you're quite sure this is all right?

DUFFY.

Perfectly sure.

STEVE.

(*Appealingly to* JUANITA.) He says—he thinks, it's all right.

JUANITA.

(*Brandishing knife.*) Dios mio!

STEVE.

Duffy, are you sure this is the man?

DUFFY.

There's no mistake about—him. That is Brooke Travers.

BOSTICK.

I am *not* Brooke Travers!

JUANITA.

(*Close at* STEVE'S *elbow.*) Well?

STEVE.

(*To* BOSTICK.) You're right—you're not Brooke Travers. I'm sorry you're not, sir, but you're not.

DUFFY.

What's that?

STEVE.

I can't help it, I feel just as bad as you do. That man is not Brooke Travers. That man is free! (*To* JUANITA.) Are you satisfied now?

JUANITA.

Yes, my friend.

DUFFY.

This is an outrage. (LUCY *runs on from anteroom left. As his back is* turned to her she does *not* recognize BOSTICK.)

LUCY.

(*To* STEVE, *in great distress.*) They told me the President had ordered you to be shot. (BOSTICK *turns toward her. She recoils.*) Arthur!

STEVE.

Arthur? Do you *know* this man?

LUCY.

This is the man I am going to marry, Arthur Bostick.

STEVE.

(*With wild delight—to* JIM.) He's mine! He's mine!
(*To* LUCY.) That isn't Arthur Bostick! That's Brooke
Travers. Why every man in New York knows Brooke
Travers. Ask any New Yorker you like. (*Points to*
JIM.) Ask that man. (*Points at* BOSTICK.) Isn't He
Brooke Travers?

JIM.

Of course he is! (STEVE *runs to desk and violently stamps
the extradition paper with the consular seal.*)

STEVE.

Of course he is! (*Shoves paper at* DUFFY.) Officer,
there is your prisoner. Take him to New York.

JUANITA.

You dare to defy me? (STEVE *in fear springs from her,
which shows her to* DUFFY.)

DUFFY.

The accomplice! I have a warrant for you, too!

STEVE.

(*Leaping back with delight.*) You have a warrant for
her? Then take her, too. Take them both to New York.
(DUFFY *seizes her wrist and with the assistance of two policemen pulls* BOSTICK *and* JUANITA *to the steps.*) Put them
in the hold of the ship—and yourself with them, and—
sink the ship!

[89]

BOSTICK.

This is an outrage, an outrage!

JUANITA.

I will have revenge—revenge! (DUFFY *and the police rush up* steps *and go off, dragging with them* JUANITA *and* BOSTICK. LUCY *is at the foot of* steps *looking after them.* STEVE *dances across the stage to table.*)

LUCY.

(*Indignantly.*) Why did you send that man to New York?

STEVE.

So that you couldn't marry him! (LUCY, *with a gesture of anger, runs off left.* STEVE *attempts to rush after her; the sentinels lock their bayonets in front of him. To soldiers.*) How dare you stop me! I am the American Consul!

CORPORAL.

El Presidente commands it.

STEVE.

The President! I made him President. Jim, bring these gentlemen some of that champagne. José, help those gentlemen. (*To* CORPORAL.) How much does the President give you to guard me?

CORPORAL.

Eighteen cents a day, but he doesn't give it.

STEVE.

Eighteen cents for a brave soldier. Why, I will give you twenty cents a day. Are there many more like you?

CORPORAL.

There are two thousand more, just as brave as I am.

STEVE.

Will they be my guard of honor, too, for twenty cents a day?

CORPORAL.

Yes, Excellency.

STEVE.

(*Shouting.*) I'll do it! I'll do it!

JIM.

What—what are you going to do?

STEVE.

(*Leaping upon table, and waving a bottle of champagne.*) I am going to start a revolution against Campos. I am going to make myself President. I will be Dictator of San Manana! (HYNE, JIM, JOSÉ, *and the soldiers raise the glasses of champagne toward* STEVE, *and cheer him wildly, waving their muskets, as the curtain falls.*)

ACT III.

Same as in Act II, except that there is now in the centre of the stage a round table. About it are set three short wooden benches. On these are seated STEVE, *the* CORPORAL, *and three other soldiers engaged most amicably in playing poker. On the table are the bottles of champagne and glasses of the Second Act. At the desk* JOSÉ *is busily writing. Everyone is smoking a huge cigar.*

STEVE.

I'll take two cards, please. (*Soldier on his left deals him two cards.*)

CORPORAL.

I'll take two cards, also.

STEVE.

You want *two* cards? Now, are you sure you understand this game?

CORPORAL.

Si, señor.

STEVE.

You're sure you want *two* cards?

CORPORAL.

Si, señor.

STEVE.

All right. Give him two cards. You can have more if you want.

CORPORAL.

No, *gracias.* (*He is dealt two cards.*)

STEVE.

Is that all, now? You took two cards, hey? Well, I'll bet five cents.

CORPORAL.

I—I raise you one peseta.

STEVE.

You raise *me*!

CORPORAL.

Una peseta.

STEVE.

Humph! Well, I'll raise you.

CORPORAL.

Well, I raise you one more time.

STEVE.

Raise me again. (*He counts the money in the pot.*) There's forty cents in that pot. I'll have to see you for the percentage. I call you.

CORPORAL.

You call me?

STEVE.

Yes. What you got?

CORPORAL.

I got three kings.

STEVE.

You *are* learning the game! You got three kings, hey? That's odd, for I have three kings too. What's your next highest card?

[93]

THE DICTATOR

CORPORAL.

My next highest card is—another king!

STEVE.

Oh, that's no good! Mine's an ace! (*As he throws down his cards the key of the wireless telegraph sounds;* STEVE *holds up his hand for silence.*) Hush! Listen! (*Calling.*) Is that you, Jim?

JIM.

(*From the bedroom.*) Yes, sir. (JIM *appears at door.*) Is it working?

STEVE.

Yes, working fine. Do it again. (JIM *exits right, and key again sounds.*) Keep it up, it sounds great. (HYNE *enters left, and with surprise halts, listening to the wireless.*)

HYNE.

Hello, who's that calling me?

STEVE.

That's Jim! (*Calling.*) Come out, Jim! (JIM *appears at door.*)

HYNE.

Jim?

STEVE.

Yes, we've tapped your machine and run a private wire into my bedroom.

HYNE.

A wire in your bedroom! What for?

STEVE.

Well, you see, some one might question the fact that I *am*

the American Consul, and it occurred to me it would be very convenient if we could call up the State Department and the State Department would answer that I am all right— —

(*Laughing.*)   Oh, I see!

No one could tell whether the answer came from the White House or my bedroom.   With the Marconi you've got to take any answer they give you, but from my bedroom you get the exact answer you want.   (*In an eager whisper.*)   Well, how did you succeed?   Have you bribed everybody?

I've bought up all the friends Campos ever had.   Every officeholder in this town is now out for *you*.

Good!

But you came near losing me.

How?

The shock I got giving away thousand-dollar bills.   I haven't quite woke up yet.

But the town's awake.

I wish you fellows were not prisoners, you could go out and see for yourselves.

[95]

STEVE.

I'm not a prisoner.   I'm a patriot.

HYNE.

Patriot!   Why, this isn't *your* country.

STEVE.

No, but I find that anyone down here who is against the government is a patriot. (*He crosses to* JOSÉ *and reads what he is writing.*)   Another proclamation?

JOSÉ.

Si, señor.

STEVE.

That's good!   Put it up in the Plaza. (JOSÉ *goes out left.   To* HYNE.) We give them proclamations fresh every hour.   Did you read the one in the Plaza?   No?   Oh, I wish you had!   I wrote that one.   I said if their warships tried to enter this harbor—my warships would sink them.

HYNE.

But *you* haven't got any warships.

STEVE.

Neither have they.   And I said, "Campos has insulted a distinguished diplomat"—that's me—"for which reason the Liberal Party will tolerate Campos no longer."

HYNE.

The Liberal Party?

STEVE.

Yes, I'm the Liberal Party.   I'll bet I'm the most liberal party this town ever saw.   The Governor alone cost me two thousand dollars.   I offered him fifteen hundred to betray the President, but he held out for two thousand. Said Campos was his dearest friend—and he couldn't do it for less. The army—that goes by contract; you pay the commanding general and he rents it out by the week. I've got it for this week. They cost me four hundred and fifty dollars. That's not dear for an army, is it? Still, even with a cheap army, I don't see what can prevent my being Dictator by lunch time. My revolution breaks loose at eleven. Now the only thing that's worrying me is that that ship hasn't sailed, and until Duffy and Juanita have started for New York I'm likely to be arrested in earnest—and to be stabbed, too.

HYNE.

Well, if you want to get rid of the ship, why don't you sign those papers?

STEVE.

No! that ship can't leave with John T. Bowie on board. Before she sails I want *him* on shore.

HYNE.

What are you going to do with Bowie?

STEVE.

I'm undecided yet. (*Takes slip of paper from his pocket.*) Here's a copy of the message I sent him by José to lure him on shore.

HYNE.

(*Looking at paper.*) It's signed Rivas.

STEVE.

Yes; José copied Rivas's handwriting and signed Rivas's name.

HYNE.

(*Reads.*) "To-day I will be released from jail. To-

[97]

night I will again be President. Come on shore at once and receive your reward."

STEVE.

And he'll get it, too.

HYNE.

"Wait at the consulate. Rivas." That ought to fetch him, but he won't come to the consulate.

STEVE.

Yes, he will. José will tell him I'm in jail or shot—as he planned I'd be. (HYNE *goes up to wireless.*) What are you going to do?

HYNE.

I'll just telegraph the ship and find out if Bowie has left it. (*He works the key of wireless, receiving answer during following speech.*)

STEVE.

Good! Everything is coming my way now. I've got rid of Duffy and Juanita and Bostick—my hated rival. Now, if Bowie will walk only into my parlor.

HYNE.

(*Having received message.*) It's all right. Second officer says Bowie and his wife left the ship ten minutes ago.

STEVE.

(*Down at desk.*) Fine! Now, then, I'll seal the ship's papers (*picks up ship's papers from desk and begins to stamp them with consular seal*), and you send the Captain a wireless and tell him he can weigh anchor in ten minutes. (HYNE *works the wireless.* STEVE *stamps the papers violently.*) Good-by, Mr. Duffy, good-by!

SOLDIER.

(*Off left.*) *Halto!*

DUFFY.

(*Off left in a* tone *of* terror.) Don't stop me! I'm a secret service detective.

STEVE.

Duffy! (DUFFY *rushes on left with clothes muddy and torn and eyes blackened. He throws himself in front of* STEVE *and clasps him around the knees. The two soldiers follow him from left, and* CORPORAL *and the other soldier come down from* centre.)

DUFFY.

Save me! Protect me! I claim the protection of the American Consul!

STEVE.

(*Shaking him off.*) Save *you*! Where are your prisoners?

DUFFY.

They're not my prisoners. I was *their* prisoner.

STEVE.

What have you done with Brooke Travers?

DUFFY.

That wasn't Brooke Travers. He was the man he said he was—a missionary from the mountains——

STEVE.

Nonsense!

DUFFY.

I'm convinced of it! (*He rises.*)

JIM.

Who convinced you?

DUFFY.

About a hundred of his parishioners—each with a machete *that* long.

[99]

HYNE.

Where?

DUFFY.

At the Market Place. About a hundred mountaineers shouted out "*El Padre!*" and he yelled, "To the rescue my children!" They chased me all the way to the hotel with that Juanita woman in front with a knife—that long. She swears she'll have my heart's blood. Hide me, please hide me——

STEVE.

(*With disgust.*) Bah! Are you afraid of a woman?

DUFFY.

I *am*! And she swears she'll have *your* heart's blood, too!

STEVE.

My heart's blood.

DUFFY.

She's coming now to get it.

STEVE.

(*To soldiers.*) Here! What do you mean hanging around doing nothing? Guard those doors! (*Soldiers run off left and centre.*) Don't let anybody get in! Heavens! here am I paying for a whole army and I'm not safe from that woman yet.

DUFFY.

Well, I'm not safe either. Can't you hide me some place?

STEVE.

No! Yes, I have it. Go hide yourself on the steamer. She sails in ten minutes. Go back to New York. You will be safe there. (*Pushes him left.*) I shall be so sorry to part with you, Duffy, but it's your only chance to escape.

DUFFY

No!

STEVE.

Your life is in danger.   If Juanita catches you——

DUFFY.

I won't leave this place until I have arrested Brooke Travers.

STEVE.

(*Crosses and whispers* to HYNE.)   Hyne, I wonder if we could persuade him that Bowie is Brooke Travers.

HYNE.

I guess so.

STEVE.

You'll help me, won't you.

HYNE.

Sure, I will.

STEVE.

Jim——

JIM.

Colonel.

STEVE.

Go back to the hotel and bring that criminal here with Mrs. Bowie, and tell Mrs. Bowie I'm in jail.

JIM.

Yes, sir.   (*Exit* centre.)

DUFFY.

Why do you want your wife to think you're in jail?

[101]

STEVE.

(*Startled.*) My wife!

DUFFY.

I don't see why——

STEVE.

(*He glances meaningly at* HYNE.) That's it, Duffy, *you* don't see why. (*To* HYNE.) He—he—wouldn't see why—would he?

HYNE.

(*Mysteriously.*) Ah, no!

STEVE.

But *we—we* see why!

HYNE.

Yes—we see why!

STEVE.

Duffy, *you* are *happily* married.

DUFFY.

Yes, sir.

STEVE.

Your wife *loves* you, Duffy.

DUFFY.

Yes, sir.

STEVE.

(*To* DUFFY.) But suppose she did *not*, Duffy. Suppose she loved a villain—a—viper. Suppose she refused to come on shore and share your home, and planned to fly with the viper to Jamaica on that very steamer, Duffy, would you not hide your sorrow from such a wife—even in a jail?

DUFFY.

No, I don't think I would. I'd *make* her come home.

STEVE.

But she has ceased to love me, Duffy. And what is home without love? She has loved that viper ever since we left New York, when he rushed up the gangplank, pale and trembling, and begged me to conceal him in my cabin. "Hide me!" he cried, "the police are on my track."

DUFFY.

(*Excitedly.*) The police?

STEVE.

Ah! I should not have told you that. I promised him I would not betray him.

HYNE.

Oh, go on and tell him! Why should *you* shield *him*?

STEVE.

I promised him. I even tried to sacrifice that young missionary in order that *he* might escape.

DUFFY.

Look here, gentlemen, you're keeping something back from me. I demand the name of that man.

STEVE.

No. Cruelly as he has wronged me, I will not tell you his name.

DUFFY.

That's enough! You don't have to! I know his name!

STEVE AND HYNE.

(*Admiringly.*) You do?

DUFFY.

I worked it out by deductions.

[103]

HYNE.

Isn't he wonderful!

STEVE.

What folly for us to try and hide anything from that man. He frightens me. He reads my very soul.

DUFFY.

(*Producing handcuffs.*) There'll be no mistake this time.

STEVE.

Ah, spare him, Duffy! I cannot forget that my wife loves him. Let those poor guilty souls go free. What's ten thousand dollars to you?

DUFFY.

Ten thousand dollars!

STEVE.

(*Impatiently.*) Yes, the reward the New York police offered for him—dead or alive. (HYNE *to conceal his smile turns up stage.*)

DUFFY.

Have the New York police offered ten thousand dollars for that fellow?

STEVE.

Dead or alive.

DUFFY.

(*Explosively.*) I don't care who he is! He goes back to New York!

HYNE.

(*At centre looking off right.*) Look out! He's coming!

DUFFY.

(*Excitedly.*) I call on you two to help me arrest this man.

STEVE.

Not that, Duffy, not that!

DUFFY.

Yes, in the name of the law. (STEVE *and* DUFFY *hide on right of centre door,* HYNE *on left.* BOWIE *enters centre, following* JIM *coming from right.*)

JIM.

(*Speaking as he* enters.) No, sir, Campos put him in jail an hour ago.

DUFFY.

Now then! (*From behind him* DUFFY, STEVE, *and* HYNE *each seize* BOWIE's *arms and* DUFFY *handcuffs his hands behind his back.*) Run, get me a cab! (JIM *runs off left.*) You are my prisoner, Mr. Brooke Travers. (MRS. BOWIE *enters centre.*)

BOWIE.

(*Struggling violently with handcuffs.*) Brooke Travers! What does this mean? Take those things off me! (*Turns and sees* STEVE.) You! Oh, so you did this!

DUFFY.

(*Eagerly.*) No, *he* didn't—I did it all myself. I get all the reward.

MRS. BOWIE.

(*Clinging to* BOWIE. *Hysterically.*) John! John! what does this mean?

BOWIE.

(*To* DUFFY.) Take these things off me. I am the American Consul.

STEVE.

Pardon me, *I* am the American Consul.

[105]

DUFFY.

(*To* BOWIE.) Of course he is; you told me so yourself.

BOWIE.

(DUFFY *and* HYNE *drag* BOWIE *to the* steps.) I will appeal to the President.

STEVE.

Who made him President? I did. Officer, take him to New York.

BOWIE.

(*Struggling.*) I'll be hanged if I go to New York.

STEVE.

So will I. (BOWIE *is now on steps.*)

MRS. BOWIE.

John! they will have to arrest me, too. I will never desert you. (DUFFY *endeavors to separate them.*)

DUFFY.

Now, madam, now—madam!

MRS. BOWIE.

Don't touch me, you monster!

DUFFY.

Madam, I am not speaking to you officially, but as a family man, married eight years. Before it is too late, go back to the husband you promised to honor and obey. (*Points at* STEVE.)

MRS. BOWIE.

To *that* man! That brute!

DUFFY.

(*Beseechingly.*)   Now, do, Mrs. Bowie.

STEVE.

No, it's too late, Duffy, old friend, let her go.   She has chosen that man, let her go with him.   (*To* MRS. BOWIE.) You never loved me, Kittie—Julia.

MRS. BOWIE.

No, I certainly never did.

STEVE.

Oh, you hear that, Duffy?

DUFFY.

(*Horrified.*)   She admits it!   (JIM *appears at door left.*)

JIM.

The cab's ready, sir.

DUFFY.

Good!   Come on, now!   (*Pushes* BOWIE *up* steps.)

BOWIE.

(*To* STEVE.)   You think you're mighty smart, don't you, but I took five thousand dollars from you.

STEVE.

You took my wife from me.   That's worth five thousand. (MRS. BOWIE *turns suddenly and screams at him.*)   It's worth fifty thousand.   (DUFFY *rushes off with* BOWIE *and* MRS. BOWIE, *assisted by* JIM. *Eagerly to* HYNE.) Do you think Duffy can get him to New York?

HYNE.

Didn't you tell Duffy if he got him there he'd have ten thousand dollars?

STEVE.

Yes.

HYNE.

He'll get him there.

STEVE.

But Bostick got away from Duffy.

HYNE.

Yes, but he had Juanita to fight for *him*.

STEVE.

Juanita! Heavens! I'd forgotten her. And she's coming here for my heart's blood. I'll never get my revolution started if they don't leave me alone. (*Looks at watch.*) It's to break out at eleven, and it's twenty minutes to that now.

CORPORAL.

(*At centre, looking off right.*) Excellency, here comes a woman. Do I shoot?

STEVE.

Yes, shoot her.

HYNE.

(*Looking off right to* CORPORAL.) No, stop! (*To* STEVE.) It's Miss Sheridan.

STEVE.

Miss Sheridan! (*Enter* LUCY *and* JOSÉ.)

LUCY.

I saw Mrs. Bowie come in here. Could I speak to her? (HYNE *indicates* STEVE—*she turns.*)

STEVE.

Can I do anything for you?

LUCY.

Señor José says that at the hotel I'm in danger.

STEVE.

In danger?

JIM.

Colonel—Colonel!

STEVE.

Well!

JIM.

Juanita! I've just seen her at the hotel.

JOSÉ.

Si! She is coming with a knife so long. (*Holds his hands far apart.*)

STEVE.

That knife of hers grows longer every minute. No one is safe from that woman. But don't be frightened, my guard of honor will protect you. Hyne, have you got a gun?

HYNE.

(*Touching his hip pocket.*) Yes.

STEVE.

Then go in there, please. (*Points left.*) And see she doesn't get in that way. And José, you go with him. (HYNE *and* JOSÉ *exit left. To* JIM.) Is your gun loaded?

JIM.

(*Picks up shotgun and looks down barrel.*) I think so.

STEVE.

Well, go in my bedroom and find out. Put it at your head—and pull the trigger. If it goes off—it's loaded.

JIM.

(*Crossing to door right.*) Yes, sir. (*Slaps his chest.*)
If that woman comes, you'll find *me*——

STEVE.

Under the bed; yes, I know. (JIM *exits into bedroom.
To soldiers at centre door.*) Now, don't let her slip by
you, boys.

LUCY.

(*Admiringly.*) You are very resourceful. Somehow I
feel I am safer with you than I would be with Colonel
Bowie. I don't trust *him*.

STEVE.

Do you trust me? (*From the bedroom there comes a puff
of smoke and the report of a gun.* JIM *appears at door.*)

JIM.

It *was* loaded, sir!

STEVE.

You're a bad shot. Try the other barrel. (*Exit* JIM.
To LUCY.) Do you trust *me*?

LUCY.

I'd like to, but I can't after the way you treated poor
Mr. Bostick. Oh, *why* did you say he was Brooke Travers?

STEVE.

Well, somebody had to be Brooke Travers.

JIM.

(*At door.*) Look out! Juanita's coming!

LUCY.

What shall I do?

[110]

STEVE.

(*Pushing* Lucy *behind the desk.*) Get behind me, get behind me. (JUANITA *enters from upper right leading the* CORPORAL *by the ear. At* centre *she pushes him from her and enters.*)

JUANITA.

Don't try to stop me! Where is the traitor? (JUANITA *discovers* STEVE *and* LUCY.) Ah, ha! and the girl too!

STEVE.

(*To* LUCY.) Look out! she's got a knife!

JUANITA.

Señorita, I want a word with you.

STEVE.

(*Timidly.*) How do you do? You didn't go to New York, did you?

JUANITA.

Traitor! I will have my revenge on *you* later. *You* can wait.

STEVE.

Oh, yes! I can wait. I'm in no hurry.

JUANITA.

Señorita, you wish to marry the man I love. Well, I have come to ask you *why?*

LUCY.

Why what?

JUANITA.

Why should you marry the man I love. What have you done for him, that *you* should be his wife? Have you ever saved him from a jail; have you brought him food

[111]

when he starved; have you, with your knife in hand, fought for him in the public street?

LUCY.

I certainly have not!

JUANITA.

(*Scornfully.*) No, not *you*! not *you*!

STEVE.

You see, where she comes from young ladies who fight in the streets find it difficult to get anybody to marry them.

JUANITA.

You are a child, you are afraid, *you* should marry a man (*points contemptuously at* STEVE) like *that*——

STEVE.

Yes, just like me. That's what I've been telling her.

LUCY.

Madam, what right have you to question me about Mr. Bostick?

JUANITA.

What right? Because I love him. I would go with him to the end of the world.

STEVE.

Well, there's a steamer leaving in just ten minutes——

JUANITA.

And if you want Arthur Bostick for your husband you will have to fight for him.

STEVE.

Oh, well, that settles it! If we have to fight for him, we don't want him, do we? We'll let him go.

LUCY.

Pardon me, madam, but I cannot discuss my engagement with you.

JUANITA.

Very well. (*Goes up* centre.) Then you shall discuss it with Mr. Bostick in my presence. He is at the hotel. I will bring him here, and he shall choose between us. (*Exits* centre.)

LUCY.

Oh! this is intolerable! How dare she bring him here to choose between us? I won't bear it! It is humiliating, insulting. I have come all the way down here to marry Mr. Bostick because my *conscience* told me to, and now he can't make up his mind whether he wants to marry me or somebody else. If he doesn't make up his mind soon, *I* will.

STEVE.

That's the way to talk! That's splendid! You're a girl after my own heart. That is, I wish you were. I've suspected several young ladies of being after my own money but no one has ever cared for my heart, and it's all yours—and you don't want it. (*Sadly.*) Oh, how different things might have been, if they'd only been different!

LUCY.

(*Gently.*) In what way different?

STEVE.

Oh, if you could only have cared for me—and if Campos wasn't going to shoot me on sight, and if I could go back home without going to jail.

LUCY.

(*Incredulously.*) To jail? You?

STEVE.

Miss Sheridan, I have deceived you outrageously. If you knew the truth you would despise me.

LUCY.

No, Mr. Steve——

STEVE.

My name's not Steve. I'm Brooke Travers myself!

LUCY.

Brooke Travers!

STEVE.

(*Alarmed.*) Hush! Don't let anybody know it. Down here they think I'm Colonel Bowie.

LUCY.

Why do they think you are Colonel Bowie?

STEVE.

I guess I must have told them. I bribed Bowie to let me take his name. You despise me. You're right. But I swear to you, Miss Sheridan, that the only thing of which I have been certain since I left New York was that I love you more than any other woman I ever knew.

LUCY.

Don't, please don't, Mr. Steve! I'm sorry.

STEVE.

Only sorry?

LUCY.

Don't think it's easy for *me*. I promised—and I've kept my promise. I'm here! Two thousand miles from my home, and Mr. Bostick is ashamed to show his face.

STEVE.

No he isn't, here he comes now. (*Enter* BOSTICK *and* JUANITA.) Now, Mr. Bostick, this is a great crisis in your life and I want to advise you.

BOSTICK.

I can't see that you have any interest in this.

STEVE.

I haven't. That's the reason my advice is so valuable. If you want a wife who never will bore you, I advise you to choose Juanita.

BOSTICK.

Thank you, but I promised Miss Sheridan. My conscience——

STEVE.

Never mind your conscience. Think of your heart— remember, Juanita saved you from jail.

BOSTICK.

You're right.

JUANITA.

Arthur, I'm waiting.

BOSTICK.

Juanita, will you be my wife?

LUCY.

(*With delight.*) I'm free! Free!

STEVE.

I congratulate you, Bostick.

BOSTICK.

Thank you. Juanita will make an ideal wife for a missionary. She will persuade many of the natives to enter my church.

STEVE.

If she persuades them the way she persuaded me, I bet they enter your church on the run.

JUANITA.

(*Grimly.*) I'd like to see anyone stay out of my Arthur's church.

STEVE.

(*To* BOSTICK.) I can't see how I ever mistook you for Brooke Travers. He never could have shown the courage that you are exhibiting now. (*To* JUANITA.) My best wishes, señora. (BOSTICK crosses *to* LUCY, *who shakes hands with him.*)

JUANITA.

The same to you— Have you told her who you are?

STEVE.

Yes.

JUANITA.

And you have asked her to marry you?

STEVE.

No.

JUANITA.

It would be a brave girl who would marry an escaped criminal.

STEVE.

Well, the man who is to be your next husband is no coward.

[116]

BOSTICK.

We would be happy, Consul, if you would add the joy of your countenance to our wedding breakfast.

STEVE.

I'm sorry, but if I go outside of the consulate I will be shotted.

BOSTICK.

I'm sorry! Good-by! (BOSTICK *exit centre.*)

JUANITA.

Wait for me, Arthur! *Señorita*, let me advise you the next time not to wait too long to get married, as the *señoritas* here are very attractive.

LUCY.

I thank you, but I prefer to remain free.

JUANITA.

If you marry that man (*points at* STEVE), you will be free in a week.

LUCY.

Free in a week?

JUANITA.

Yes, you will be his widow.

STEVE.

I've got as good a chance to live as Bostick. (*Exit* JUANITA. HYNE *rushes on left followed by four soldiers.* JIM *appears left.*)

HYNE.

Colonel, Campos is returning for you.

STEVE.

Campos!

HYNE.

With a hundred soldiers.

STEVE.

I'm paying for those soldiers.

HYNE.

Yes, but he has them.

STEVE.

(*To* LUCY.) You must go back to the hotel. Quick!

LUCY.

No, I won't leave you when you are in trouble.

STEVE.

Then you'll never leave me, for I'm always in trouble. But now, please go.

LUCY.

(*Moving to chair below desk.*) No, I will not.

STEVE.

Very well, then give me moral support. I need it. (*To soldiers.*) Here! You're not a guard of honor now. No, I'm your prisoner. You're keeping me prisoner. Take away that barricade, Jim; hide that shotgun. Look innocent everybody, look innocent. Look as though you never heard of a revolution. (*Outside left are heard cries of "Viva el Presidente! Viva! Viva!"* CAMPOS *enters left accompanied by officer and two soldiers who remain on top step. After his entrance orders of command are heard from outside, suggesting the presence of a large number of troops. The* CORPORAL *and the three other soldiers raise their rifles to* CAMPOS *in salute.* CAMPOS *looks with some surprise at* LUCY, *and bows stiffly. Then to* STEVE.)

CAMPOS.

Well, Colonel Bowie, I have found you out.

STEVE.

No, you find me in. Naturally, with soldiers at each door——

CAMPOS.

I have read your proclamation in the Plaza. I come myself to take you to El Morro prison.

STEVE.

Oh, I think not! Not this American Consul. When my President hears of this——

CAMPOS.

Your President—he will never hear of it.

STEVE.

(*Points off to harbor.*) Won't he? I'll send him a report by the *Bolivar.*

CAMPOS.

The *Bolivar* has sailed for Jamaica with Sergeant Duffy and his prisoner. (*Slowly and impressively.*) No, you will not send a report by that ship. No one will ever hear from you again. My post office will not receive your letters, no steamers will be permitted to carry one. And at Puerto Banos we have no cable. You may cry out for help, but the four walls of a dungeon carry no sounds. (STEVE, *overwhelmed by the solemnity of this sentence, for a short time stands stupefied. His eyes turn helplessly from* LUCY *to* HYNE, *until finally they rest upon the wireless. He smiles exultingly.* HYNE, *following the direction of his eyes, comprehends, and they approach and silently shake hands.* LUCY *is puzzled.* JIM *remains unmoved.*)

STEVE.

(*To* CAMPOS.) Yes, you're right about a dungeon cell being a poor transmitter. But my government is an up-to-date government and every Consul's office nowadays is fitted up with one of those! (*Points at wireless.*)

CAMPOS.

The wireless! You can talk—with him!

STEVE.

I can talk with him or her or anybody I want to. What do you suppose I keep it for? Why—I've had that working overtime ever since you put me under arrest. I've had New York on the wire since——

CAMPOS.

New York! Oh no! oh no! You cannot, how you say? —pull the blind over my eyes. New York is two thousand miles away.

STEVE.

Pardon me, I said *the New York*——

CAMPOS.

Yes, I know, the City of New York—two thousand miles——

STEVE.

No, no, the battleship *New York*—ten thousand tons.

CAMPOS.

You talk—with that—to a battleship.

STEVE.

I've been talking all morning to the whole Caribbean squadron. There are four battleships, six cruisers, and a dozen torpedo boats. (*To* HYNE.) Hyne, where was that squadron when we called it up last?

HYNE.

I think—it was about——

STEVE.

About twenty miles off shore, wasn't it?

HYNE.

Yes, about twenty, or possibly twenty-one.

STEVE.

Yes, perhaps twenty-one, and they were coming this way at fifteen knots an hour, weren't they? At full speed, I think you said.

HYNE.

Full speed, and cleared for action.

STEVE.

(*Looking off at door centre toward harbor.*) Why, I believe the torpedo boats are coming in now.

CAMPOS.

(*Running to window upper left.*) No, no, you do not. *I* do not see them.

STEVE.

Of course you can't *see* them. They are submarines. (*To* HYNE.) You might just call them up again to convince the President that they really are coming. (*To* JIM *impressively.*) Jim, go into my bedroom—and—bring me my cigar case.

JIM.

Yes, sir. (*Exit door right.*)

STEVE.

(*In a whisper to* LUCY.) I have a private wire into that room. Jim sends the answers. (*To* CAMPOS.) Will you have a cigar, General?

CAMPOS.

(*Nervously, with his eyes turned toward the wireless.*) No, *gracias,* I have not the appetite.

STEVE.

Hyne, just call up the Admiral. (HYNE *solemnly works the key of the wireless.*)

CAMPOS.

The Admiral! Which Admiral is that?

STEVE.

There is only one "the" Admiral—sit down and you will hear him talk to me. (CAMPOS *and his officer sit on bench left, while* HYNE *works the key. There is a pause.* HYNE *stops, and* STEVE *listens complacently for the reply.*) Now, you'll hear how it works. (*After a longer pause,* STEVE *glances uneasily toward the door right, and coughs.* HYNE *looks off right and coughs more violently.*)

CAMPOS.

(*To his officer.*) The Admiral—I think he is asleep! (*He laughs jeeringly.*)

OFFICER.

Si, Excellency, *si.* (*They both laugh.*)

HYNE.

(*Nervously.*) Now, General, there's quite a little fog

out there; in a fog the electric waves don't vibrate as quickly——

STEVE.

And icebergs—several icebergs, they're always in the way when you——

CAMPOS.

(*To the officer.*) Icebergs! In the tropics! Yes, ha! ha! (*They laugh.*)

STEVE.

(*Sternly.*) You might just repeat that message, Hyne. Hurry him up a bit; speak sharply to him. I don't care if he is the Admiral, he's no right to keep a Consul waiting.

HYNE.

No, certainly not. (*Works key, while he looks anxiously at door right.*) Hello! Hello! Hello!

STEVE.

(*With confidence.*) That will fetch him, I think. Now you wait and you'll hear him speak. (*There is a pause. As no answer comes,* STEVE *shows his dismay.* JIM *enters from room right, unconcernedly carrying a cigar case. He comes down to* STEVE *and proffers it to him.*)

JIM.

Your cigars, sir.

STEVE.

You—you idiot! Cigars! What do I want with cigars?

JIM.

You *said* cigars, sir.

STEVE.

I said—I said, I want cigarettes. Keep your ears open, can't you? Listen! If you'd listen, you'd known what I do want.   Go back there and get me the Navy Plug cigarettes, the Admiral cigarettes, the Battle-ax, *battleship* cigarettes and keep your ears open.   Get out!

JIM.

Yes, sir.   (*Runs off right.*)

CAMPOS.

(*Rises.*)   Well, I have waited so long as I can.   You come with me now to El Morro.

HYNE.

(*Excitedly.*)   No, no!   (*Works key.   At the sound, CAMPOS halts uncertainly.*)

STEVE.

Take me to El Morro now?   With a squadron and the Admiral at your very gates?

CAMPOS.

(*Advances to him.*)   Bah! you make a bluff.   There is no Admiral, there is no squadron.   You are a Yankee fraud.   (HYNE *withdraws from the key.   There is a pause.   The eyes of all are turned upon the wireless.   Then the key ticks slowly in answer.   CAMPOS starts in consternation.*)

STEVE.

General—listen!

CAMPOS.

What is that?

STEVE AND HYNE.

Hush!   (*They pretend to listen.   They look at each other, nodding approvingly and smiling as though what the wireless said amused them.   They move their lips as though reading a message.*)

CAMPOS.

(*Breathlessly.*)   You understand him, eh?

STEVE.

(*Impatiently.*)   Hush! can't you?   (*The key ceases ticking.   STEVE heaves a sigh of relief, as though greatly pleased with the message.*)

CAMPOS.

What does he say?

STEVE.

What does he say?   Can't you understand the Morse alphabet?

CAMPOS.

No, what did he say?

STEVE.

(*To* HYNE, *laughing.*)   He wants to know what he said. (*They laugh, their laughter increases.*)   *You* don't want to know what he said?   (*To* HYNE.)   It was just like George, wasn't it?

HYNE.

The very image of him.

STEVE.

You could almost hear his voice?   Just the sort of thing George would say.

CAMPOS.

George?   Who is George?

STEVE.

The Admiral.   George Dewey.

CAMPOS.

Bah!   I don't believe you!

STEVE.

All right! You don't believe me, eh? Hyne, just send him one from me. (*Dictates.*) "The Admiral, on board *Olympia*, off Porto Banos." (HYNE *works keys.*) Got that? "Dear George—the President is here, the President is here"—and no, say, "the man who *was* President is here and is using threatening language." Wait! "Please throw a twelve-inch shell"—no, make it a six-inch. We don't want to blow up the whole town. "Throw a six-inch shell into the Plaza to let them know you're coming." Sign it "Bowie, Consul." (*Triumphantly to* CAMPOS.) The answer to that will be a six-inch shell.

CAMPOS.

· (*Savagely.*) And the answer to that—will be two hundred six-inch shells from the fortress of Puerto Banos! I will sink those ships! I will blow up those ships! I will fill the harbor with scrap iron!

STEVE.

(*Alarmed.*) Here, you mustn't talk in that way of an American warship; you don't appreciate your danger. You ought to be frightened.

CAMPOS.

Me, frightened! I will fight those ships until Puerto Banos lies in ruins. (*To soldiers.*) Guard that man well. (*To* STEVE.) When I have placed my soldiers on the ramparts, I will return and shoot you with my own hand. (*He draws his sword.*) In ten minutes. Unless your battleships arrive in ten minutes, you are a dead man. (*Rushes off, followed by officer, shouting.*) To the ramparts! Death to the Americans! (*Cheers, and the cry "Death to the Americans!" is heard.* STEVE, LUCY, *and* HYNE *listen in alarm. Each time the cry is repeated they jump nervously.*)

HYNE.

(*In an awed whisp*er.)   What are you going to do?

STEVE.

What can I do?   Can I evolve battleships out of thin air in ten minutes?

LUCY.

You shouldn't have frightened him.

STEVE.

Frightened *him!*   Did he act to you as though he were 'rightened. (*Points left.   To* HYNE.)   Go watch in the street, and let me know when he's coming.   (HYNE *exits left.*)

LUCY.

Now you must try to escape.   You still have seven minutes.

STEVE.

No, dear girl, even if I could escape, I couldn't leave you. (*He takes her hands and kisses them.*)   Good-by.   (*The wireless begins to tick slowly.   At the sound* STEVE *raises his head.*)   Confound that idiot!   (*Calls off right.*)   Jim, stop that noise!   (*The instrument continues to tick.*)   Stop it, there's no use doing that now, he's gone.   (STEVE *turns to* LUCY.   JIM *enters and comes down unseen by* STEVE *and* LUCY.   *The wireless continues to tick.*)   Confound that idiot!   (STEVE *turns and in amazement, sees* JIM, *and from him looks at the wireless.*)   Who's doing that?

JIM.

I don't know, sir.   I'm not.

STEVE.

(*Rushes to wireless excitedly.*)   Good heavens!   We've

hooked something! We've tapped a real wire! (*Calls off left.*) Hyne! Hyne! come here! we've got a bite, we've got a bite! (HYNE *runs on left and halts on steps, listening to the wireless.*)

HYNE.

(*Excitedly.*) Hush! That's some one calling us. (*He runs to instrument and violently works the key.*)

STEVE.

(*Hysterically.*) Don't lose him! Play him gently! Be careful! Don't let him get away from you!

HYNE.

(*Leaning over key.*) Hush, be quiet! (*The instrument ticks in answer.*)

STEVE.

Who—who is it? What's he say?

HYNE.

He's calling us up! He wants to know who we are!

STEVE.

Never mind who *we* are, find out who *he* is. Tell him we're in great danger, we want help, we want it quick. (HYNE *works the key.*) What did you say to him?

HYNE.

I asked him who he is. (*The key answers.*)

STEVE.

Who is he?

HYNE.

Hush! He's trying to tell me. (*As the instrument sounds,* HYNE's *lips move as though reading a message.*) "The—battleship—*Oregon.*"

LUCY.

(*Wildly.*)   A battleship!   We're saved!

JIM.

Hurrah!

STEVE.

(*In great excitement.*)   Keep your hand on the key.
Don't let him get away from you.

HYNE.

(*Working key violently.*)   What good can she do us?
She may be two hundred miles away.

STEVE.

Two hundred miles?   And Campos is coming back in
two minutes.   Find out where she is, can't you?

HYNE.

That's what I'm trying to do, if you'll only keep quiet.
I want to find out where she is just as much as you do.
I don't want to die. (*They all wait breathlessly for the
answer.   The key answers.* HYNE *raises his hand for
silence.*)   Hush! (*He reads message aloud.*)   "Ten minutes ago—we—landed—marines at Porto Banos." (HYNE
shouts.)   She's here *now!*

STEVE.

Hurrah! (*He embraces* JIM.   HYNE *embraces* LUCY,
and then leaps around stage, shouting and waving his hat.
STEVE *in search for marine glasses throws all the books and
papers off the desk.   With glasses he runs to centre door,
and looks toward harbor.*)   There she is!   As big as the
Flatiron Building! (*He seizes* LUCY *and waltzes with her.
Outside cheers and cries are heard.*)   "*Los Americanos!*"
"*Los Americanos!*"

CORPORAL.

(*Running on left.*) Excellency! The *Americanos*, the *Americanos!* (LIEUTENANT VICTOR *and a dozen blue jackets carrying arms run down* steps.)

LIEUT. VICTOR.

(*Saluting.*) Are you the American Consul, sir?

STEVE.

Never mind who *I* am. *You*'re here, that's the main thing. You're in charge of this office. (*Shakes his hand violently.*) And you didn't take charge a minute too soon. (*Shakes hands warmly with each blue jacket.*) How are you? How do you do? I am very glad to see you. (*Slips between two of them and takes an arm of each.*) Say, I'll never leave you fellows. Don't lose sight of me, will you?

LIEUT. VICTOR.

Your wireless was to Admiral Dewey, but we read it. I was sent ashore to protect Americans.

STEVE.

The only Americans in Porto Banos are in this room. So you just stay where you are.

LIEUT. VICTOR.

(*Saluting.*) Very good, sir. (*To the blue jackets.*) Guard that door over there—and you fall back on that one. (*Blue jackets separate and at each door stand at attention. To* STEVE.) Oh, Mr. Consul! before leaving Porto Rico, we received instructions to inquire here for an American named Duffy. Have you heard of him?

STEVE.

(*Alarmed.*) Duffy?

LIEUT. VICTOR.

Yes, Duffy—have you seen him? (*All look consciously at* STEVE. JIM *draws near him on his right.* LUCY *and* HYNE *are at writing desk.*)

STEVE.

(*Cautiously.*)   Yes, I've seen him.

LIEUT. VICTOR.

Did he say anything to you about Brooke Travers and his valet? (JIM *falls helplessly against* STEVE.)

STEVE.

(*Aside to* JIM.)   Stand up, can't you?   (*Aloud.*)   Yes, I think he did casually mention the name.

LIEUT. VICTOR.

It's a terrible affair.   Even in Porto Rico the papers are full of that murder.   (STEVE *collapses against* JIM.)

STEVE.

(*In a weak voice.*)   Then—then—it was *murder?*

LIEUT. VICTOR.

Yes, it seems that Travers and his servant got into a fight on a wharf with a cabman and a crowd of roughs. Travers had on his person twenty-five thousand dollars. That was the last time they were seen alive.   So it's pretty evident that they were both robbed and murdered.   (JIM *whispers excitedly to* STEVE.)

STEVE.

(*To* JIM.)   Be quiet!   He's trying to make us confess. It's a trap.   He's trying to make us give ourselves away. (*Turns suspiciously to* LIEUTENANT.)   But why—why, if·

these men were murdered in New York is Duffy looking for them—down here?

LIEUT. VICTOR.

Two men answering their description sailed on the *Bolivar* a few hours after the murder. Duffy was ordered here to find out if they were the men. Their *friends* sent him.

STEVE.

Their friends! Then why did he try to arrest them?

LIEUT. VICTOR.

(*Indignantly.*) *A*rrest them? The idiot! He was told to *find* them.

STEVE.

(*Eagerly.*) And—and the cabman—is he alive?

LIEUT. VICTOR.

Of course.

STEVE.

(*Wildly.*) Then if Brooke Travers was *not* murdered, could he come to life again without being hanged?

LIEUT. VICTOR.

Certainly.

STEVE.

Jim, we've been murdered for two weeks, and we didn't know it.

LIEUT. VICTOR.

What do you mean? Who *are* you?

STEVE.

I am Brooke Travers, and this—is my murdered valet. (*Stiffly.*) Simpson, you can come to life now.

[132]

THE DICTATOR

JIM.

Thank you, Colonel.

STEVE.

Not Colonel now—Mr. Travers.

JIM.

Yes, Mr. Travers.

LIEUT. VICTOR.

But I thought *you* were Colonel Bowie!

STEVE.

It's a long story. I thought I was going to be killed, and I— (*Outside there is a sudden sound of firing, shouts and cries of "Viva, viva* BOWIE!" LIEUTENANT *draws his sword and motions blue jackets left.*) "*Viva* Bowie!"— why— (*Suddenly.*) That's *my* revolution! (*Looks at watch.*) To the minute! To the minute! (*To* LIEU-TENANT.) Sir, in me you now see the President and Dictator of San Manana.

LIEUT. VICTOR.

(*Gravely saluting* STEVE.) As the representatives of the United States, we recognize your government.

STEVE.

That's the fastest recognition on record. That beats Panama. (*Takes* LUCY *in his arms.*) Lucy, I will go home. If I must be a dictator, I prefer to do my dictating to a stenographer in little old New York.

CPSIA information can be obtained
at www.ICGtesting.com
Printed in the USA
BVHW081533210119
538277BV00020B/818/P